CONTEÚDO DIGITAL PARA ALUNOS
Cadastre-se e transforme seus estudos em uma experiência única de aprendizado:

CB015098

1
Entre na página de cadastro:
https://sistemas.editoradobrasil.com.br/cadastro

2
Além dos seus dados pessoais e dos dados de sua escola, adicione ao cadastro o código do aluno, que garantirá a exclusividade do seu ingresso à plataforma.

4484432A5693896

3
Depois, acesse:
https://leb.editoradobrasil.com.br/
e navegue pelos conteúdos digitais de sua coleção **:D**

Lembre-se de que esse código, pessoal e intransferível, é valido por um ano. Guarde-o com cuidado, pois é a única maneira de você acessar os conteúdos da plataforma.

Editora do Brasil

BRINCANDO
COM INGLÊS

2

ENSINO FUNDAMENTAL
ANOS INICIAIS

RENATO MENDES CURTO JÚNIOR
Licenciado em Letras
Certificado de proficiência em Língua Inglesa pela Universidade de Michigan e TOEFL
Autor de livros de educação a distância
Professor de Língua Inglesa e Portuguesa na rede particular de ensino desde 1986

ANNA CAROLINA GUIMARÃES
Licenciada em pedagogia
Especialista em Educação Infantil e anos iniciais
Especialista em neuropsicopedagogia
Coordenadora pedagógica de Educação básica

CIBELE MENDES
Mestre em Educação
Licenciada em Pedagogia
Certificado de proficiência em Língua Inglesa pela Fluency Academy
Coordenadora pedagógica de Educação Infantil aos Anos Finais do Ensino Fundamental

Editora do Brasil

Dados Internacionais de Catalogação na Publicação (CIP)
(Câmara Brasileira do Livro, SP, Brasil)

Curto Júnior, Renato Mendes
  Brincando com inglês 2 : ensino fundamental : anos
iniciais / Renato Mendes Curto Júnior, Anna Carolina
Guimarães, Cibele Mendes. -- 5. ed. -- São Paulo :
Editora do Brasil, 2024. -- (Brincando com)

  ISBN 978-85-10-09500-6 (aluno)
  ISBN 978-85-10-09501-3 (professor)

  1. Língua inglesa (Ensino fundamental)
I. Guimarães, Anna Carolina. II. Mendes, Cibele.
III. Título. IV. Série.

24-193761   CDD-372.652

Índices para catálogo sistemático:

1. Língua inglesa : Ensino fundamental 372.652
Eliane de Freitas Leite - Bibliotecária - CRB 8/8415

© Editora do Brasil S.A., 2024
Todos os direitos reservados

Direção-geral: Paulo Serino de Souza

Diretoria editorial: Felipe Ramos Poletti
Gerência editorial de conteúdo didático: Erika Caldin
Gerência editorial de produção e design: Ulisses Pires
Supervisão de design: Aurélio Gadini Camilo
Supervisão de arte: Abdonildo José de Lima Santos
Supervisão de revisão: Elaine Silva
Supervisão de iconografia: Léo Burgos
Supervisão de digital: Priscila Hernandez
Supervisão de controle e planejamento editorial: Roseli Said
Supervisão de direitos autorais: Luciana Sposito

Supervisão editorial: Carla Felix Lopes e Diego Mata
Edição: Graziele Arantes Mattiuzzi, Sheila Fabre, Natália Feulo, Danuza D. Gonçalves e Nayra Simões
Assistência editorial: Igor Gonçalves, Julia do Nascimento, Natalia Soeda e Pedro Andrade Bezerra
Revisão: 2014 Soluções Editoriais, Alexander Siqueira, Andréia Andrade, Beatriz Dorini, Gabriel Ornelas, Jonathan Busato, Júlia Castelo Branco, Maisa Akazawa, Mariana Paixão, Martin Gonçalves, Rita Costa, Rosani Andreani e Sandra Fernandes
Pesquisa iconográfica: Maria Santos e Selma Nagano
Tratamento de imagens: Robson Mereu
Projeto gráfico: Caronte Design
Capa: Caronte Design
Imagem de capa: Thais Castro
Edição de arte: Camila de Camargo e Marcos Gubiotti
Ilustrações: André Aguiar, Carolina Sartório, Clara Gavilan, Dayane Raven, Desenhorama, DKO Estúdio, Evandro Marenda, Ilustra Cartoon, Luiz Lentini, Maíra Nakazaki, Marcelo Azalim, Marcos de Mello, Reinaldo Rosa, Saulo Nunes Marques e Vinicius Meneghin
Editoração eletrônica: Abel Design
Licenciamentos de textos: Cinthya Utiyama, Ingrid Granzotto, Renata Garbellini e Solange Rodrigues
Controle e planejamento editorial: Ana Fernandes, Bianca Gomes, Juliana Gonçalves, Maria Trofino, Terezinha Oliveira e Valéria Alves

5ª edição / 1ª impressão, 2024
Impresso na Hawaii Gráfica e Editora

Editora do Brasil
Avenida das Nações Unidas, 12901
Torre Oeste, 20º andar
São Paulo, SP – CEP: 04578-910
Fone: + 55 11 3226-0211

www.editoradobrasil.com.br

abdr
ASSOCIAÇÃO BRASILEIRA DOS DIREITOS REPROGRÁFICOS
Respeite o direito autoral

APRESENTAÇÃO

Querido aluno, querida aluna,

Este material foi elaborado para que você aprenda inglês de forma divertida, por meio de atividades estimulantes e desafiadoras, com o intuito de transformar a sala de aula em um espaço para praticar a língua inglesa brincando!

Nesta nova versão do **Brincando com Inglês**, cada aula será uma nova experiência, e você não vai querer parar de aprender. Vamos começar?

Os autores

CONHEÇA SEU LIVRO

Boas-vindas à nova edição do **Brincando com Inglês**!

LET'S START!
No início de cada volume, esta seção resgata conhecimentos prévios e apresenta atividades lúdicas que possibilitam a preparação para os novos conteúdos.

VOCABULARY
Apresenta o vocabulário das palavras vistas na unidade, com a tradução em língua portuguesa.

COMPREHENSION
As atividades desta seção visam à compreensão do texto visto na abertura da unidade.

GOOD DEED
Apresenta atividades temáticas de cunho social e ético relacionadas ao assunto de cada unidade. Aborda as competências gerais e socioemocionais da BNCC e as atividades feitas em grupo ou em dupla.

LET'S PLAY
Seção relacionada aos conceitos propostos e à temática da unidade. Você encontrará atividades lúdicas, como diagrama de palavras, jogos de relacionar, jogos de erros, desafios etc.

LET'S LISTEN

Seção com atividades que têm como objetivo a compreensão de áudios.

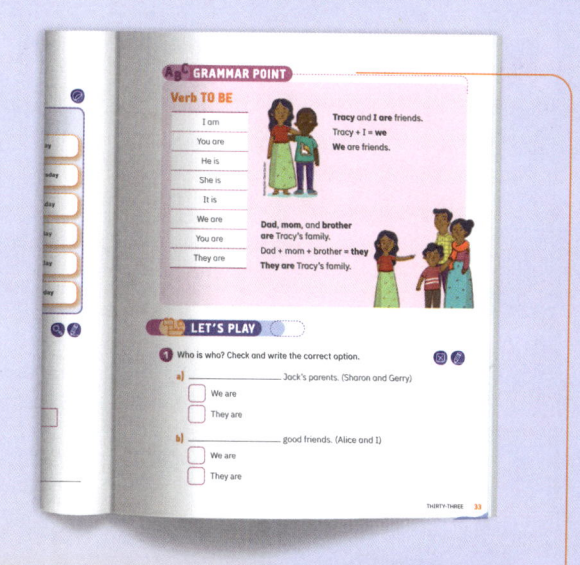

GRAMMAR POINT

Boxe com conteúdos gramaticais para que você compreenda a estrutura estudada e sistematize escrita e oralidade.

LET'S SING!

Músicas para os alunos cantarem e praticarem o vocabulário visto na unidade de forma lúdica e divertida.

STICKERS

Adesivos para colar em algumas atividades.

CELEBRATIONS

Encartes com atividades relacionadas a datas comemorativas.

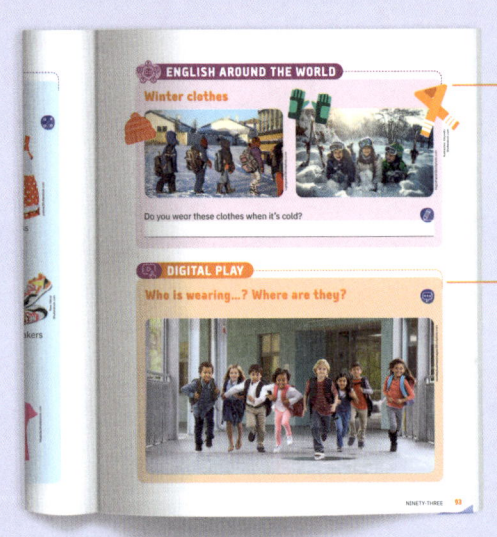

ENGLISH AROUND THE WORLD
Seção que contempla a dimensão intercultural da língua inglesa, trabalhando elementos da cultura em que se fala o idioma como língua oficial ou franca. Também são estudados os aspectos interculturais de outros países.

DIGITAL PLAY
Seção que traz atividades em que se usa a tecnologia: filmagem, fotos, uso de *apps* e jogos *on-line*.

LET'S HAVE FUN
Localizada no final das unidades, contém atividades variadas cuja proposta é desenvolver o estudo da língua inglesa na prática, ampliando o conhecimento e o vocabulário trabalhado.

AFTER THIS UNIT I CAN
Seção de autoavaliação e acompanhamento processual pelo aluno e pelo professor.

ÍCONES

- ADESIVO
- APONTAR
- CANTAR
- CARTONADO
- CIRCULAR
- COLAR
- COLORIR
- CONTAR
- DESENHAR
- ENCONTRAR/PESQUISAR
- FALAR OU CONVERSAR
- LIGAR/RELACIONAR
- MARCAR
- RECORTAR
- TRAÇAR/ESCREVER

CONTENTS

LET'S START! 8

UNIT 1
New classmates 19

UNIT 2
Friends and family 29

UNIT 3
A visit to the zoo 39

UNIT 4
The birthday party 49

UNIT 5
Let's cook! 61

UNIT 6
The little farm 73

UNIT 7
At the shop 87

UNIT 8
My city 97

REVIEW 107

PICTURE DICTIONARY 120

INDEX

   SONGS 128

   LISTENINGS 128

CELEBRATIONS 129

STICKERS 145

LET'S START!

1 Match the clothing items. Then write the names of the body parts.

My body, my clothes

T-shirt

Pants

Sneakers

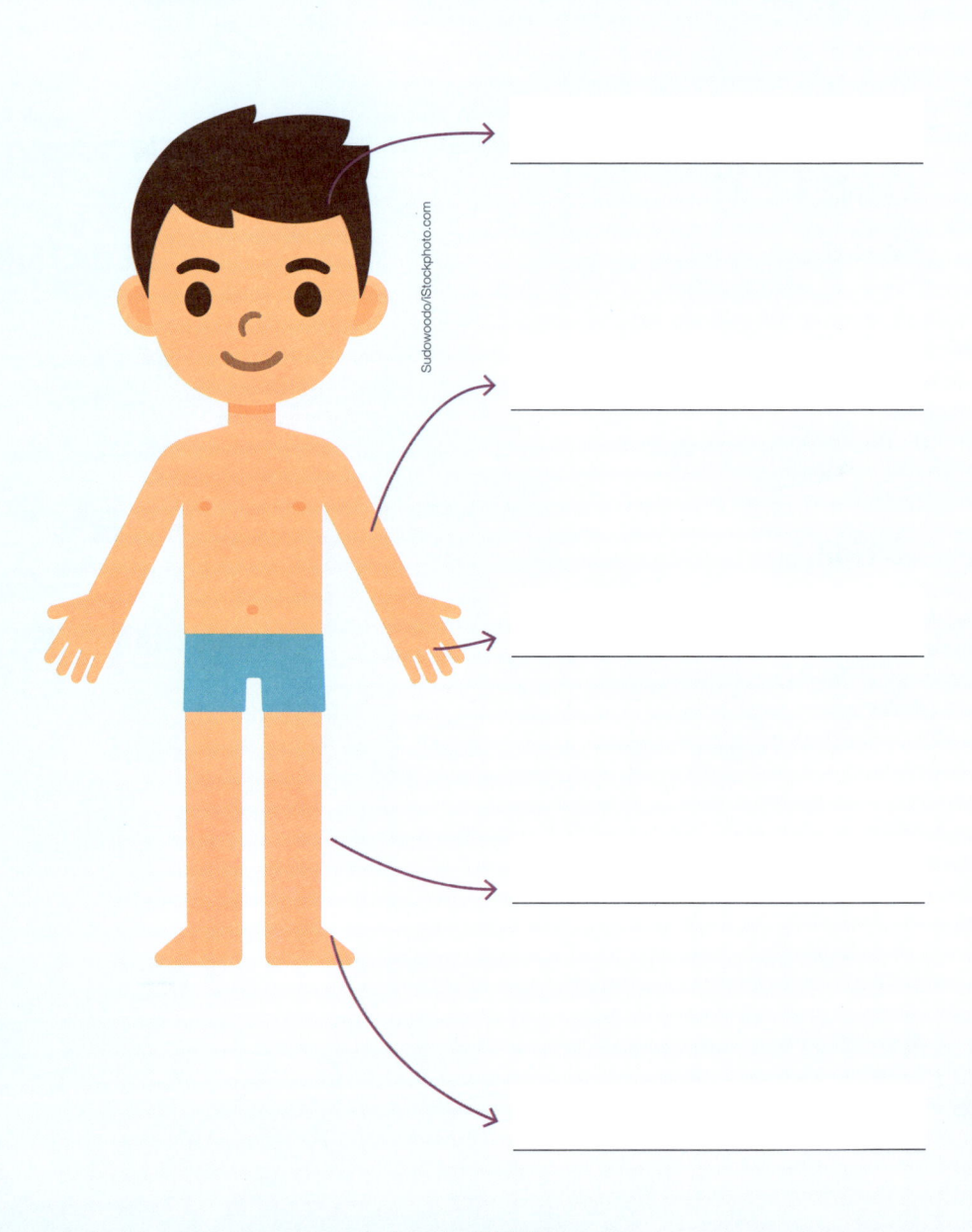

_____

_____

_____

_____

_____

2 Color the clothing items according to the color code.

Color	Clothes	Color	Clothes	Color	Clothes
🔴	T-shirt	🟢	Skirt	⚫	Shorts
🔵	Pants	🟠	Shoes	🟡	Socks
🟣	Dress	🟤	Shirt	⚪	Cap

3 Read the sentences and check.

a) It's a cat.

b) It's a rabbit.

c) It's a turtle.

4 Look at the animals. Write their names in the crosswords.

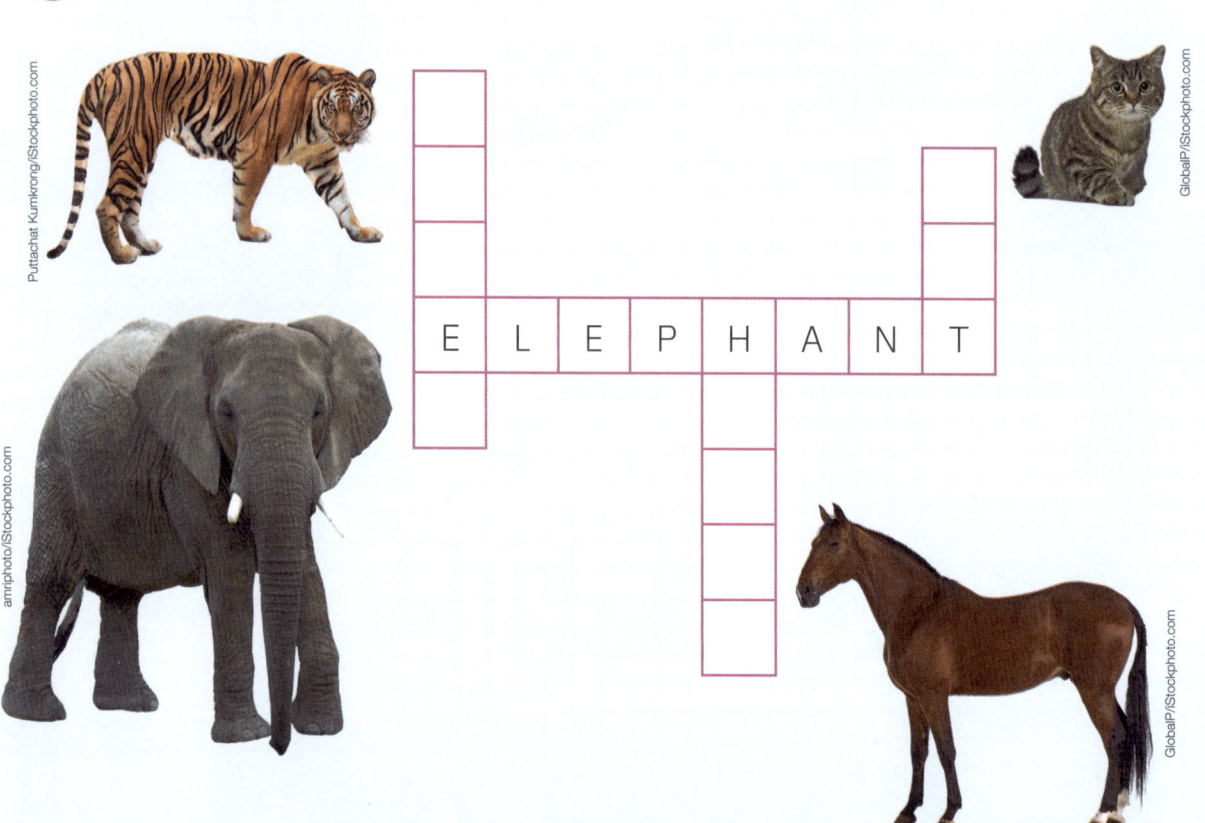

E L E P H A N T

5 Complete the sentences with the words from the boxes.

Good morning!

Good afternoon!

Good night!

a) _____ Have good dreams.

b) _____ Do you want to have breakfast with me?

c) _____ Would you like to go to the shopping mall with me?

6 Complete the sentences according to the pictures.

a)

b)

c)

d)

7 Read, find, and write the name of the family members.

a) _____

b) _____

c) _____

d) _____

e) _____

f) _____

g) _____

h) _____

i) _____

THIRTEEN 13

8 Read and color the pictures accordingly.

- Red
- Brown
- Blue
- Yellow
- Orange
- Gray
- Green

My bike is blue and yellow.

My ball is orange.

My skate is red and green.

My rope is gray and brown.

14 FOURTEEN

9 Match each word to its corresponding picture.

a) Rice

b) Meat

c) Salad

d) Pasta

e) French fries

f) Sandwich

g) Beans

h) Soup

i) Ice cream

10 Paste the stickers to complete what is missing in each scene. Then write the objects.

Bathroom

a) _____ and _____.

Living room

b) _____ and _____.

11 How many? Find and count the school objects. Then, write.

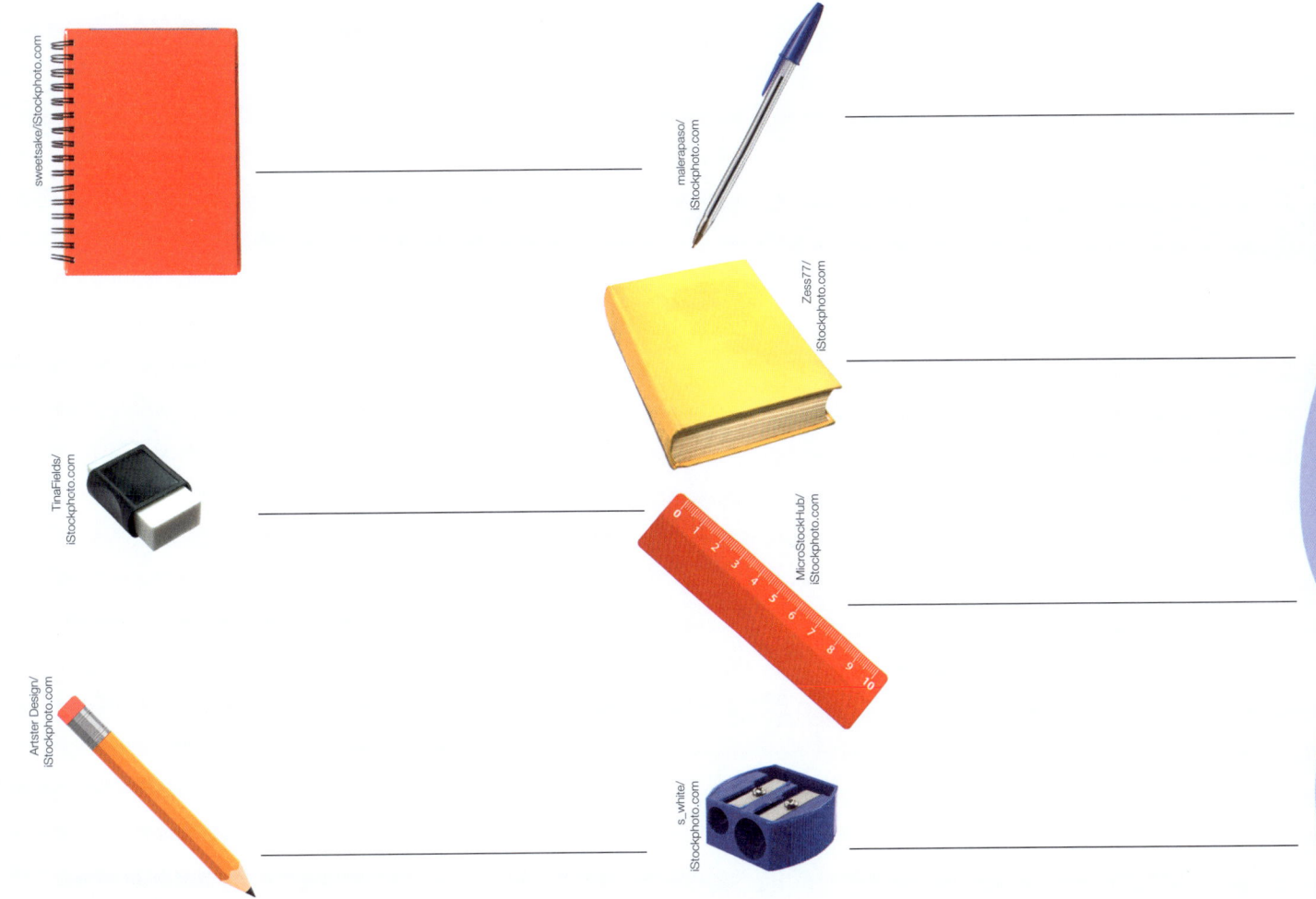

SEVENTEEN 17

12 Identify and color the corresponding shape.

Square:

Triangle:

Rectangle:

13 Make a drawing. Use a circle, a rectangle, and a triangle.

UNIT 1
NEW CLASSMATES

Good morning, class. We have a **new classmate**. **Her name is** Sarah.

Sarah, **would you like** to say **a few words**?

Hello **everyone**. My name is Sarah and I'm **happy to be here**.

Good morning, Sarah!

Welcome, Sarah!

VOCABULARY

A few: algumas.
Classmate(s): colega(s) de classe.
Everyone: todos.
Happy: feliz.
Her name is: o nome dela é.

New: novo.
To be here: estar aqui.
Word(s): palavra(s).
Would you like: você gostaria.

COMPREHENSION

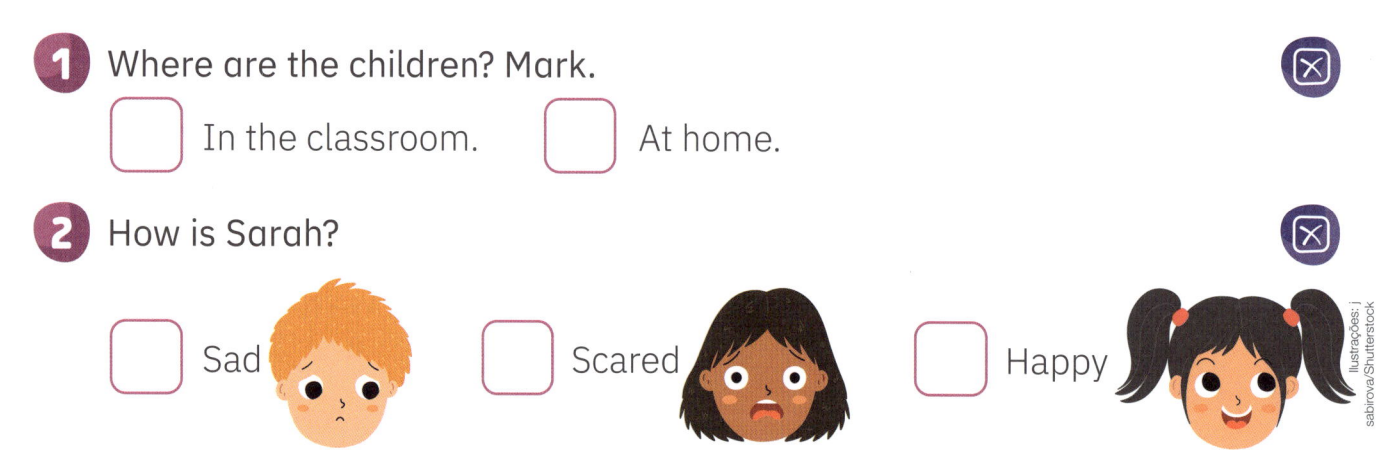

1 Where are the children? Mark.

☐ In the classroom.   ☐ At home.

2 How is Sarah?

☐ Sad   ☐ Scared   ☐ Happy

3 Let's do a role-play.

- Hi! My name's Angela. What's your name?
- Hello! My name's Gerry.
- Nice to meet you, Gerry.
- Nice to meet you too, Angela.
- How are you, Angela?
- I'm fine, thanks!

LET'S LISTEN

1 Today is the first day of school. Listen to the conversation and complete the blanks.

Isaac • Alex • Gerry

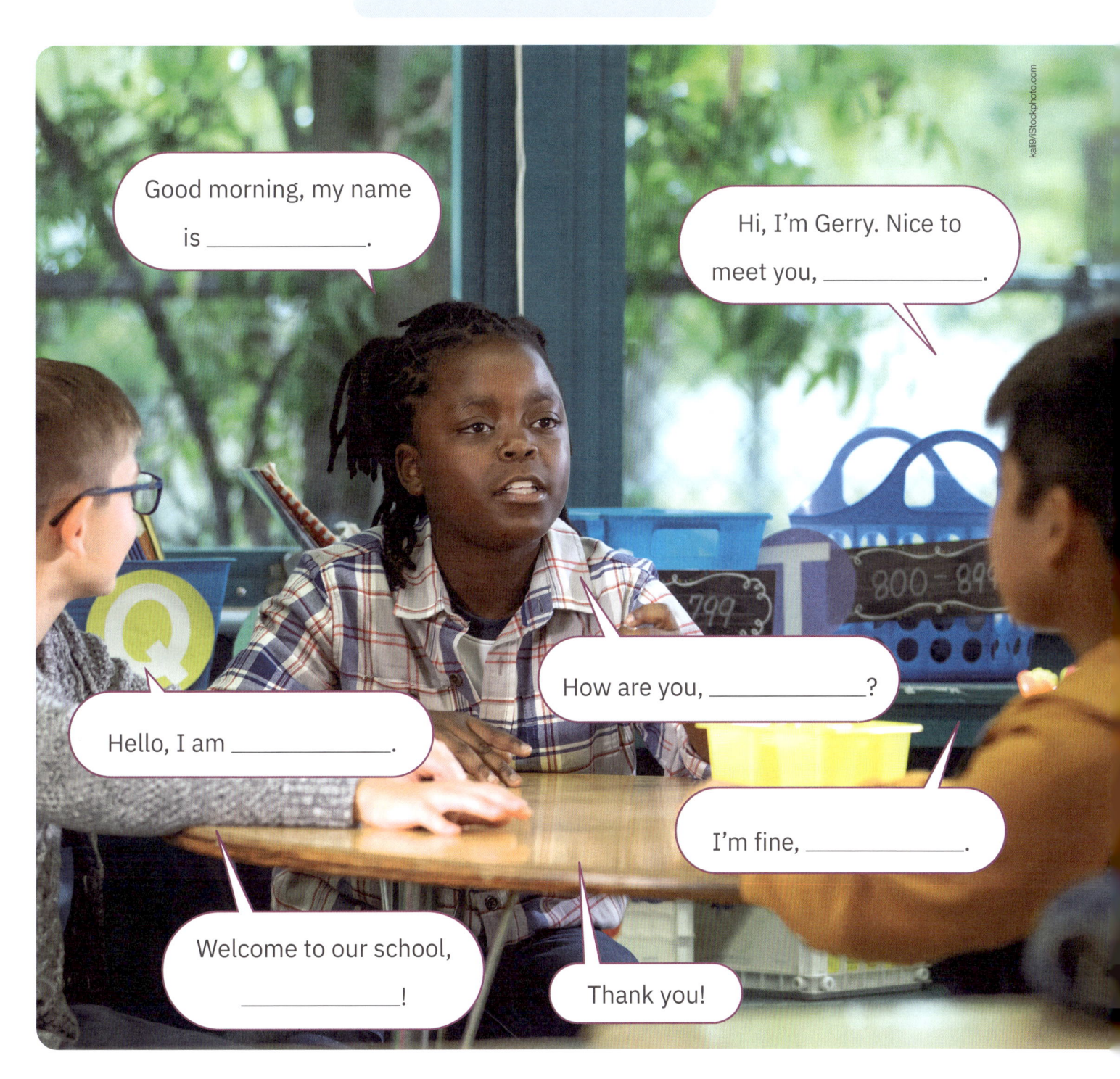

Good morning, my name is _____.

Hi, I'm Gerry. Nice to meet you, _____.

Hello, I am _____.

How are you, _____?

I'm fine, _____.

Welcome to our school, _____!

Thank you!

LET'S PLAY

1 Help Jack complete the crossword with the greetings from the box.

Hello * Good morning * Hi * Welcome

M O R N I N G

2 Match the columns to the corresponding answer.

Hey!					I'm fine. And you?

How are you?				My name's Laura.

What's your name?			Hi! How are you?

ABC GRAMMAR POINT

Verb TO BE

She **is** ⟶ Ela **é** / Ela **está**

He **is** ⟶ Ele **é** / Ele **está**

She is Alice. She is my friend.

He is Justin. He is my friend.

LET'S PLAY

1 Complete the sentences. Use the appropriate subject pronoun and its form of the verb **to be**.

This is Kate. _____ my friend.

This is Jonah. _____ my friend.

TWENTY-THREE 23

2 Look at the school building and paste the stickers in the correct place. Use the words below.

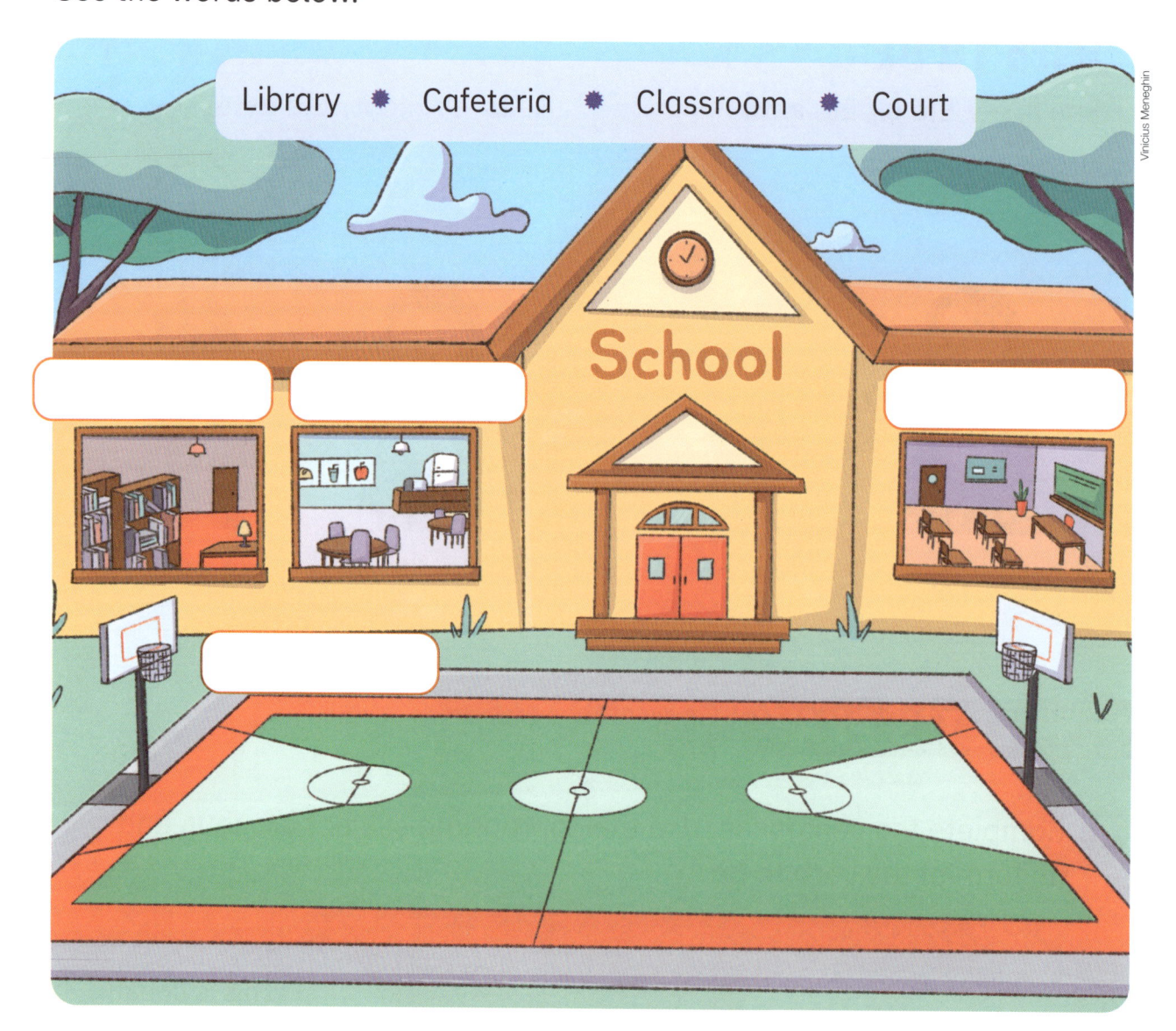

Library • Cafeteria • Classroom • Court

3 Read the tips below and guess the name of the school place.

Tip 1: It is a big place.

Tip 2: You can play sports in this place.

Tip 3: You can see the Physical Education teacher there.

The school place is the _____.

ENGLISH AROUND THE WORLD

Harry Potter's school in Atlanta (the United States)

Let's create a greeting rule in our classroom!

GOOD DEED

A clean school is everyone's responsibility!

Make a **campaign** about the importance of a clean school.

LET'S LISTEN

1 Listen to the dialogue and complete the information about each school.

BLUE BIRD SCHOOL
- 5 _____
- 1 _____
- 1 _____

LION SCHOOL
- 15 _____
- 2 _____
- 1 _____
- 1 _____

LET'S SING!

This is the way we laugh and play...

This is the way we laugh and play
Laugh and play, laugh and play
This is the way we laugh and play...
So early in the morning.
This is the way we run and jump
Run and jump, run and jump
This is the way we run and jump...
So early in the morning.
This is the way we go to school
Go to school, go to school
This is the way we go to school...
So early in the morning.

Traditional song. Adapted.

VOCABULARY

Early: cedo.
Jump (to jump): pulamos (pular).
Laugh (to laugh): rimos (rir).
Play (to play): brincamos (brincar).
Run (to run): corremos (correr).
Way: forma, modo.

DIGITAL PLAY

Nice to meet you!

Draw yourself and answer the question.

What is your name?

What is your name?

My name is Justin.

My name is _____.

AFTER THIS UNIT I CAN

- Greet others, ask questions and answer them.
- Identify school places.
- Participate in dialogues in playful activities.
- Understand that rules for coexistence are important in all kinds of school.

UNIT 2
FRIENDS AND FAMILY

Alice has a big **family**. She lives with her **dad**, her **mother**, and her **brother**. Today they are eating outside Alice's house. Alice's **grandpa**, **grandma**, **aunt**, **uncle**, and **cousins** are there. Grandpa Richard loves to cook for his **relatives**.

VOCABULARY

Aunt: tia.
Brother: irmão.
Cousin(s): primo(s).
Dad: pai.
Family: família.
Grandma: vovó.
Grandpa: vovô.
Mother: mãe.
Relative(s): parente(s).
Uncle: tio.

TWENTY-NINE

COMPREHENSION

1 Underline the words you listen.

Alice has a **big** / **small** family.

Richard loves to **cook** / **book** for his relatives.

2 Mark the correct sentences.

☐ Richard is Alice's brother.

☐ They are eating outside Alice's house.

☐ Alice has a mother and a father.

☐ Alice has a small family.

3 Look at the family chart. Is your family similar or different?

LET'S LISTEN

1 Listen and write the days of the week. Then color the image of Tracy's family having fun on a Sunday.

1.
2.
3.
4.
5.
6.
7.

LET'S PLAY

1 Complete the chart with the stickers in the correct place.

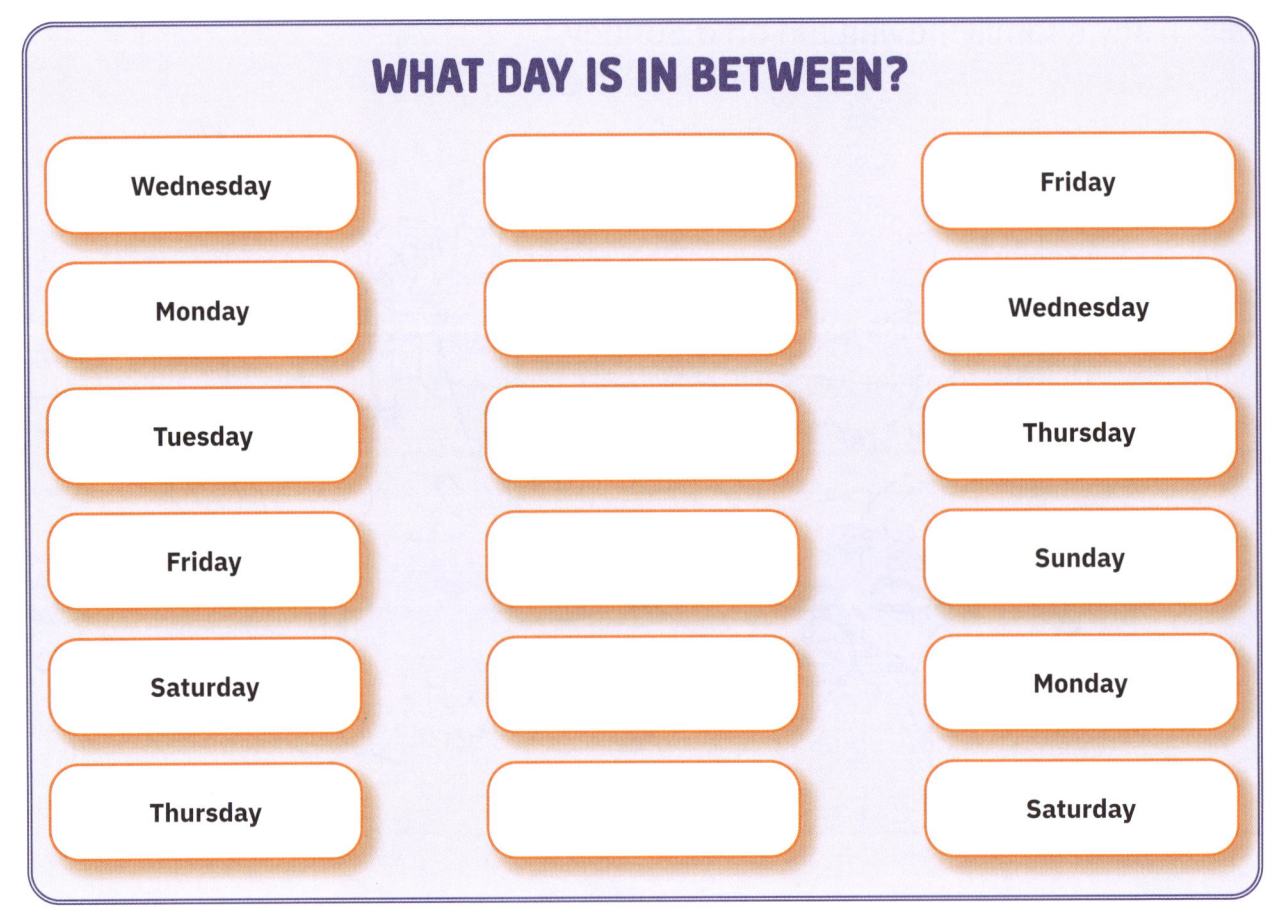

WHAT DAY IS IN BETWEEN?

Wednesday		Friday
Monday		Wednesday
Tuesday		Thursday
Friday		Sunday
Saturday		Monday
Thursday		Saturday

2 Complete the crossword.

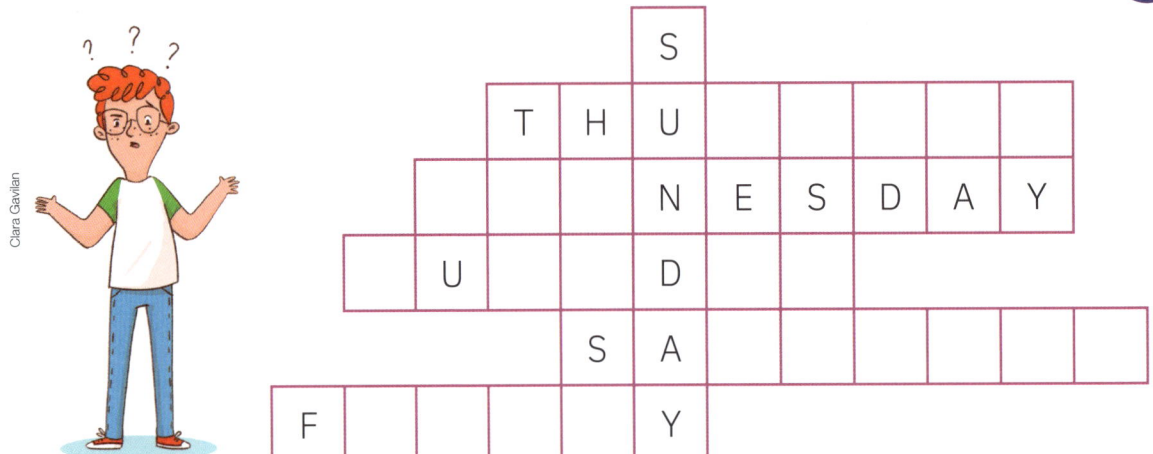

```
            S
      T H   U
          N E S D A Y
        U   D
          S A
      F       Y
```

3 What day of the week is not in the crossword?

32   THIRTY-TWO

ABC GRAMMAR POINT

Verb TO BE

I am
You are
He is
She is
It is
We are
You are
They are

Tracy and **I are** friends.
Tracy + I = **we**
We are friends.

Dad, **mom**, and **brother are** Tracy's family.
Dad + mom + brother = **they**
They are Tracy's family.

LET'S PLAY

1 Who is who? Check and write the correct option.

a) _____ Jack's parents. (Sharon and Gerry)
- ☐ We are
- ☐ They are

b) _____ good friends. (Alice and I)
- ☐ We are
- ☐ They are

2 Match the words to the correct form of the verb **to be**.

I
You
He
She
It
We
You
They

am
is
are

3 Look at the pictures. Write **we are** or **they are**.

a) _____ friends.

b) _____ friends.

34 THIRTY-FOUR

GOOD DEED

Helping in family. Everybody must help with house chores!

Look at the chart. Complete it with the chores you do at home.

- Take care of my pet.
- Keep my toys in order.
- Make my bed.
- Wash the dishes.

Helping at home

MONDAY	TUESDAY	WEDNESDAY	THURSDAY	FRIDAY	SATURDAY	SUNDAY

DIGITAL PLAY

What is the meaning of my name?

Name _____

Origin _____

Meaning _____

Enter Your First Name:

Days of the week

Days of the week, *snap* *snap*
Days of the week, *snap* *snap*
Days of the week, days of the week,
Days of the week, *snap* *snap*.
There's Sunday and there's Monday
There's Tuesday and there's Wednesday
There's Thursday and there's Friday
And then there's Saturday
Days of the week, *snap* *snap*
Days of the week, *snap* *snap*
Days of the week, days of the week,
Days of the week, *snap* *snap*.

Traditional song.

LET'S SING!

VOCABULARY

Snap (to snap): estale (estalar).
There is (there's): há (haver, existir).
Week: semana.

ENGLISH AROUND THE WORLD

The origin of the names of the weekdays

Day Name Origins

_____	: Sun + Day
_____	: The Moon's Day
_____	: Day of War
_____	: Day of Speed
_____	: Day of Thunder
_____	: Day of Love
_____	: Saturn's Day

LET'S LISTEN

1 Who are they? Listen and write.

Hello! My name is Jack and this is my _____.

a) Sharon: _____
b) Aaron: _____
c) Paul: _____
d) Suzy: _____
e) Oscar: _____

f) Jessica: _____
g) Cecile: _____
h) Vincent: _____
i) Melvin: _____

LET'S HAVE FUN

Let's play with puppets!

AFTER THIS UNIT I CAN

Greet each other.

Talk about family.

Identify different kinds of family formations.

Identify and name the days of the week.

UNIT 3
A VISIT TO THE ZOO

The children are **visiting** the zoo.

Wow! This **tiger** is **beautiful**!

Look! The **elephant** is **eating**!

Nice!

VOCABULARY

Alligator: jacaré.
Beautiful: bonito.
Eating (to eat): comendo (comer).
Elephant: elefante.
Monkey: macaco.
Nice: legal.
Tiger: tigre.
Visiting (to visit): visitando (visitar).

COMPREHENSION

1 Look at the pictures and answer the question.

Alligator

Elephant

Monkeys

Tiger

Where can you see these animals in the city?

2 Complete the sentences using the words below.

tiger • bananas • water • elephant

a) The monkeys are eating _____.

b) The _____ is gray.

c) The _____ is black, white, and beige.

d) The alligator likes _____.

LET'S PLAY

1 Complete the number pyramid.

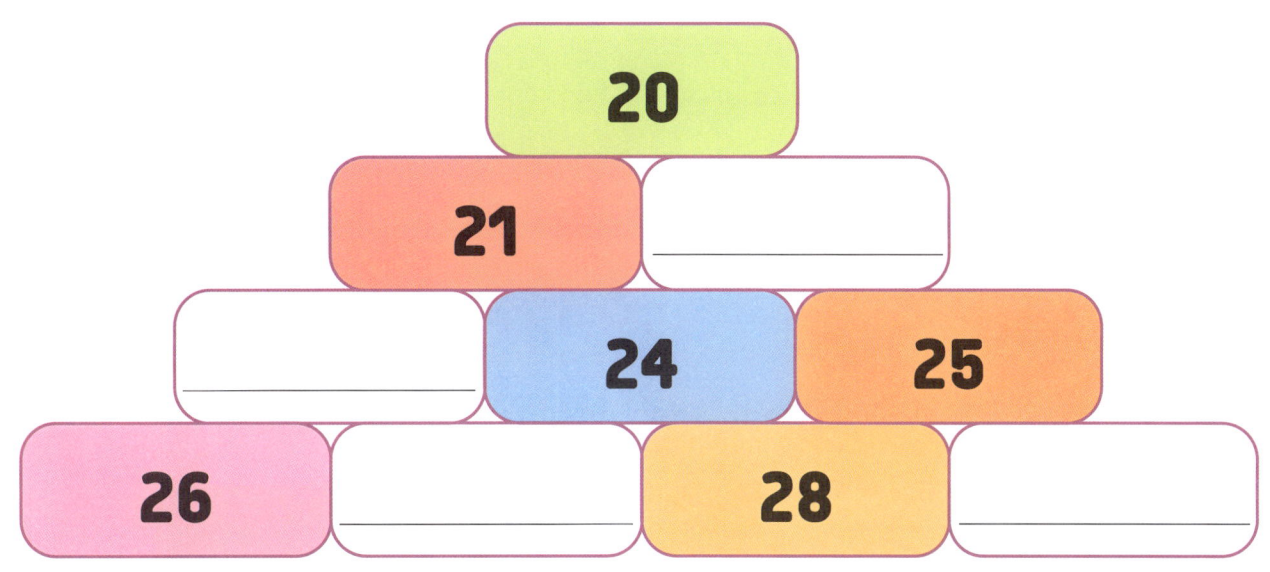

```
        20
     21     ___
  ___   24    25
26   ___   28   ___
```

2 How many wild animals can you see? Count and color the charts.

3 Complete the words and find the names of the animals.

a) all ____ g ____ tor

b) z ____ br ____

c) g ____ r ____ ff ____

d) m ____ nk ____ y

e) l ____ on

f) el ____ ph ____ nt

4 Look at the pictures. Write the names of these animals.

a) _____

b) _____

c) _____

d) _____

e) _____

f) _____

LET'S LISTEN

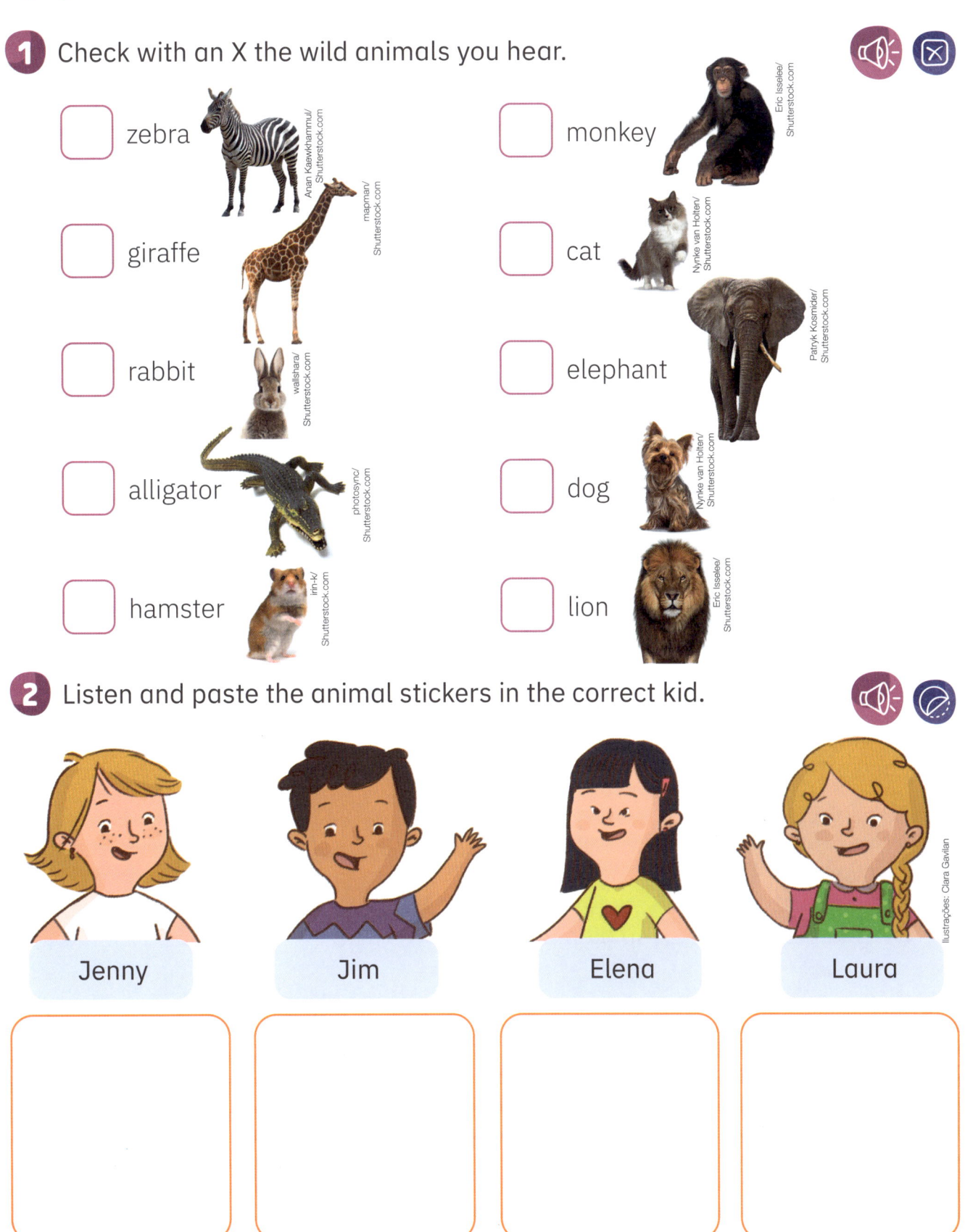

1 Check with an X the wild animals you hear.

- ☐ zebra
- ☐ giraffe
- ☐ rabbit
- ☐ alligator
- ☐ hamster

- ☐ monkey
- ☐ cat
- ☐ elephant
- ☐ dog
- ☐ lion

2 Listen and paste the animal stickers in the correct kid.

Jenny	Jim	Elena	Laura

FORTY-THREE 43

ABC GRAMMAR POINT

Verb TO BE

It is ⟶ ele ou ela **é** / ele ou ela **está**
Used for things and animals.

It **is** a giraffe. It **is** tall.

It **is** a bicycle.

LET'S PLAY

1 What animal is it? Answer using **It is**.

a) _____ an elephant.

b) _____ a giraffe.

c) _____ a monkey.

d) _____ a lion.

GOOD DEED

The environment needs the animals

Make a poster and write a sentence here to put on it.

Let's preserve the animals!

DIGITAL PLAY

Write down the folder presentation sentences.

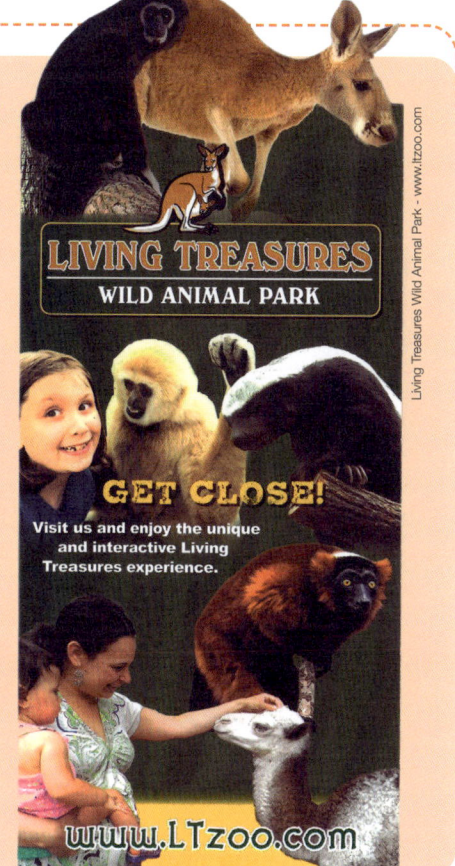

LET'S SING!

The elephant has a great big trunk

The elephant has a **great big trunk**
That goes swinging to and fro.
And he has **tiny**, tiny eyes
That show him where to go.
His great big ears
Go **flopping**, flopping
While his great big **feet**
Go **stomping**, stomping, stomping, stomping.

Folk rhyme.

VOCABULARY

Big: grande.
Feet: pés.
Flopping (to flop): movendo-se de maneira relaxada e sem direção.
Great: notável.
Stomping (to stomp): pisando (pisar) com força.
Tiny: muito pequeno.
Trunk: tromba.

ENGLISH AROUND THE WORLD

Zoos in the world

Circle the wild animals in the signs.

LET'S PLAY

1 Look at the image and write the name of your favorite animal.

AFTER THIS UNIT I CAN

- Answer questions about animals.
- Identify numbers from 20 to 29.
- Identify and use verb *to be*.
- Identify wild animals.
- Understand the importance of zoos and caring for these animals around the world.

UNIT 4
THE BIRTHDAY PARTY

Hey, Jim! I'd like to invite you to my birthday party.

How nice! When and where is the party?

It's next Saturday at my house. We'll have a cake, balloons, candies, *piñata*, and lots of fun!

VOCABULARY

Balloon(s): balão(ões).
Birthday: aniversário.
Cake: bolo.
Candy(ies): doce(s).
Fun: diversão.

Invite (to invite): convidar.
Lots of: muita.
Next: próximo(a).
Party: festa.
Would ('d) like: gostaria.

COMPREHENSION

1 Who is the birthday person?

☐ Judy   ☐ Jim

2 The invitation is to...

☐ a graduation party.   ☐ a birthday party.

3 Read and complete Judy's invitation.

Saturday * Judy's house * Jim

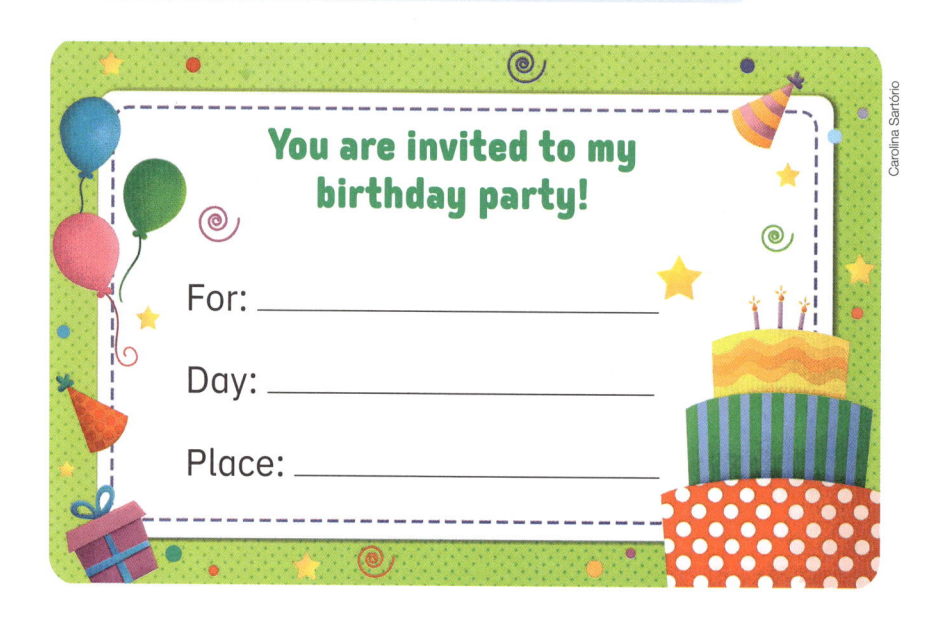

You are invited to my birthday party!

For: _____

Day: _____

Place: _____

LET'S LISTEN

1 Listen and paste the stickers.

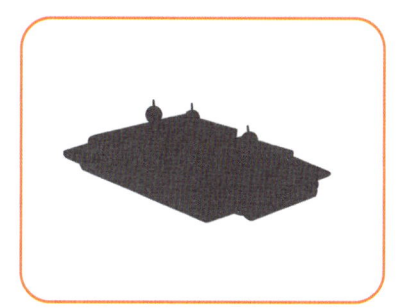

1. Candies
2. Cake
3. Sandwiches
4. Popcorn
5. Juice
6. Balloons
7. Candle
8. Birthday hat

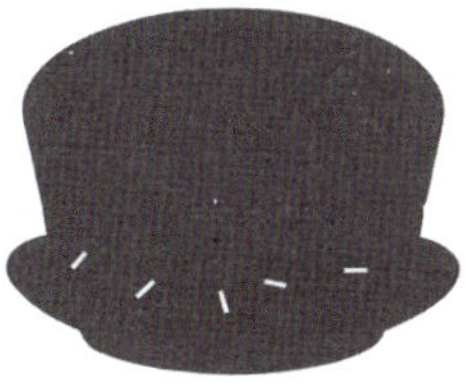

LET'S PLAY

1 Let's learn the months of the year! Say the months, color the pictures and trace the words.

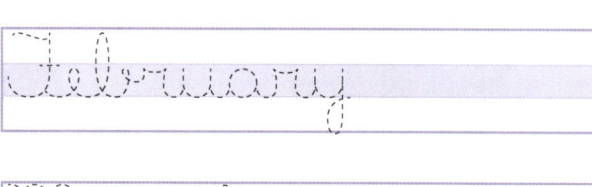

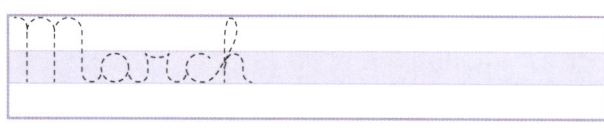

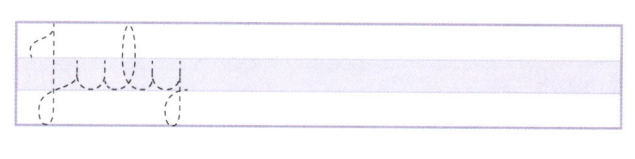

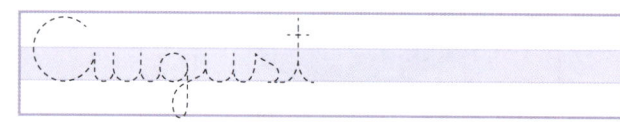

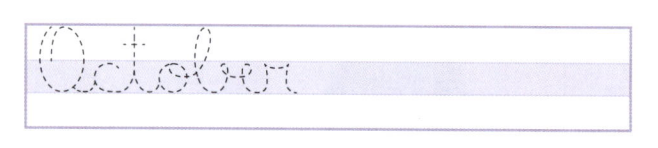

| January | February | March | April | May | June |

| July | August | September | October | November | December |

- January
- February
- March
- April
- May
- June
- July
- August
- September
- October
- November
- December

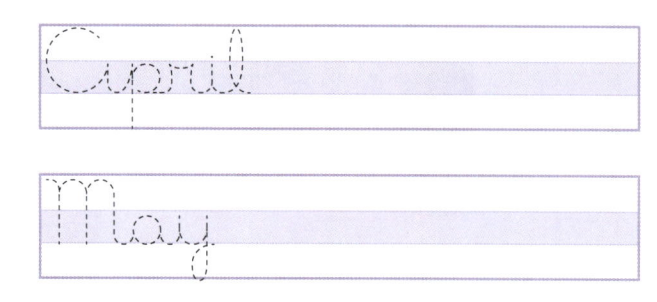

52 FIFTY-TWO

2 Write the months in the correct order.

March • January • July • October • August • February
June • December • November • April • May • September

MONTHS OF THE YEAR

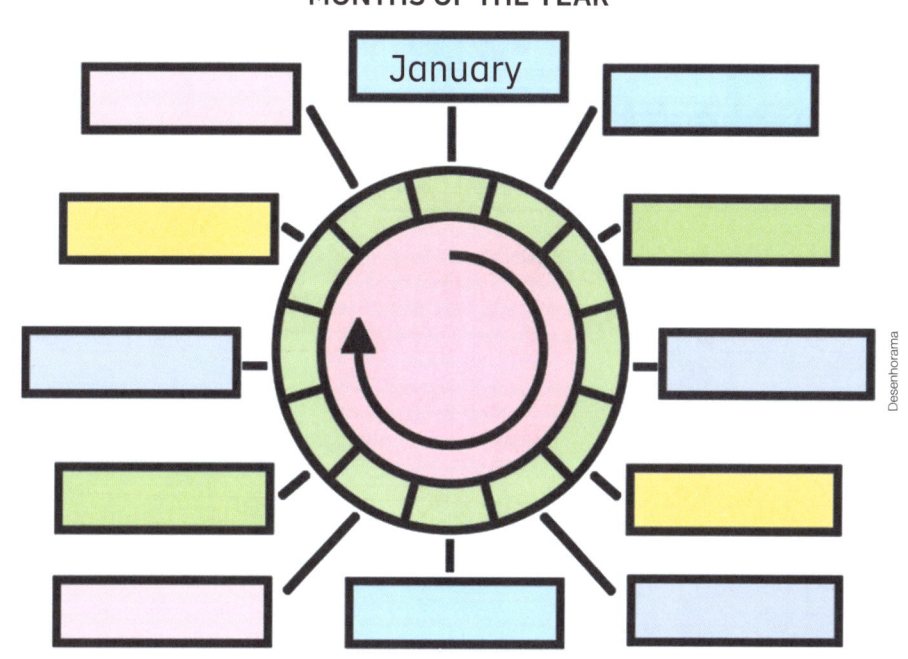

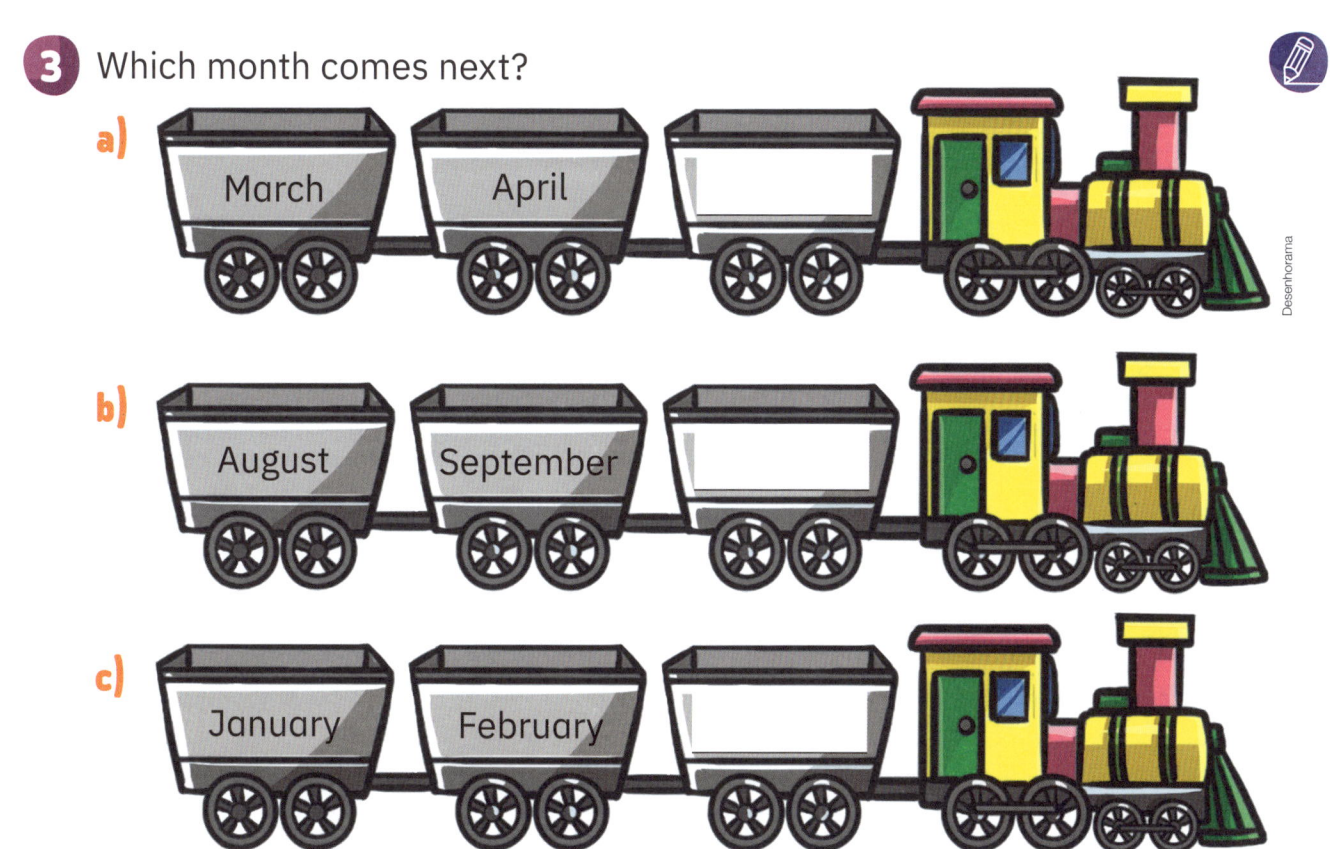

January

3 Which month comes next?

a) March, April, ___

b) August, September, ___

c) January, February, ___

LET'S LISTEN

1 Do you know how many days there are in March? Let's count!

1 one	9 nine	17 seventeen	25 twenty-five
_____ two	10 ten	18 eighteen	_____ twenty-six
3 three	_____ eleven	19 nineteen	27 twenty-seven
4 four	12 twelve	20 twenty	28 twenty-eight
5 five	_____ thirteen	21 twenty-one	29 twenty-nine
6 six	14 fourteen	22 twenty-two	30 thirty
7 seven	15 fifteen	23 twenty-three	31 thirty-one
_____ eight	16 sixteen	24 twenty-four	

2 Listen and complete the class birthday list.

Class Birthday List

January
____ Jack
____ Tracy

February
____ Melissa
____ Gerry

March
____ Paul
____ Mary

April
____ Diana
____ Justin

May
____ Ken
____ Alice

June
____ George
____ Philip

July
____ Laura
____ Bill

August
____ Judy
____ Jenny

September
____ Harry
____ Michelle

October
____ Nate
____ Angela

November
____ Elena
____ Jim

December
____ Ester
____ Jordan

LET'S PLAY

1 Circle the items with the color indicated in the box and count.

● Blue	Balloons
● Red	Birthday hat
● Green	Invitation
● Yellow	Cake

_____   _____   _____   _____

GRAMMAR POINT

Verb TO BE

I **am** ⟶ Eu **sou** / Eu **estou**

You **are** ⟶ Você **é** / Você **está**

I **am** Jim.

You **are** a student.

LET'S PLAY

1 Match the subject pronoun to the corresponding form of the verb **to be**.

a) I • are

b) You • am

2 Read Jim's message to Jenny and complete it with **am** or **are**.

Hello, Jenny!
Next Saturday is my birthday party.
I _____ having a party at 3 o'clock at my house.
You _____ invited!

Jim

ENGLISH AROUND THE WORLD

Look at the flags. Take the kids to their corresponding birthday party.

Alles Gute zum Geburtstag

Pinata Posada

GOOD DEED

Life is good. Enjoy your life!

In groups, make a poster with messages about enjoying life.

58 FIFTY-EIGHT

Happy birthday!

Happy birthday to you
Happy birthday to you
Happy birthday, **dear** friend
Happy birthday to you!
From good friends and **true**,
From **old** friends and **new**,
May **good luck** go with you,
And **happiness** too!
Happy birthday to you
Happy birthday to you
Happy birthday, dear friend
Happy birthday to you!

Traditional song.

LET'S SING!

VOCABULARY

Dear: querido(a).
Good luck: boa sorte.
Happiness: felicidade.
New: novo(a).
Old: velho(a).
True: verdadeiro(a).

FIFTY-NINE 59

LET'S HAVE FUN

Let's celebrate the birthdays of the month!

Make a list of preparations for the community birthday party.

Date	Time	Place
_____	_____	_____

Birthdays	Foods	Beverages
_____	_____	_____
_____	_____	_____
_____	_____	_____

AFTER THIS UNIT I CAN

- Identify different elements of a birthday party.
- Recognize typical birthday party food items.
- Identify cardinal and ordinal numbers from 1 to 31.
- Reflect on interesting facts about birthdays around the world.
- Understand the importance of having a positive attitude towards life.

UNIT 5
LET'S COOK!

Dinner is served! Today we have **pasta**!

I would like to eat **fish**.

I would like to have **lobster**.

I **would like** to eat **chicken**.

VOCABULARY

Chicken: frango.
Dinner: jantar.
Fish: peixe.

Lobster: lagosta.
Pasta: macarrão.
Would like: gostaria.

SIXTY-ONE **61**

COMPREHENSION

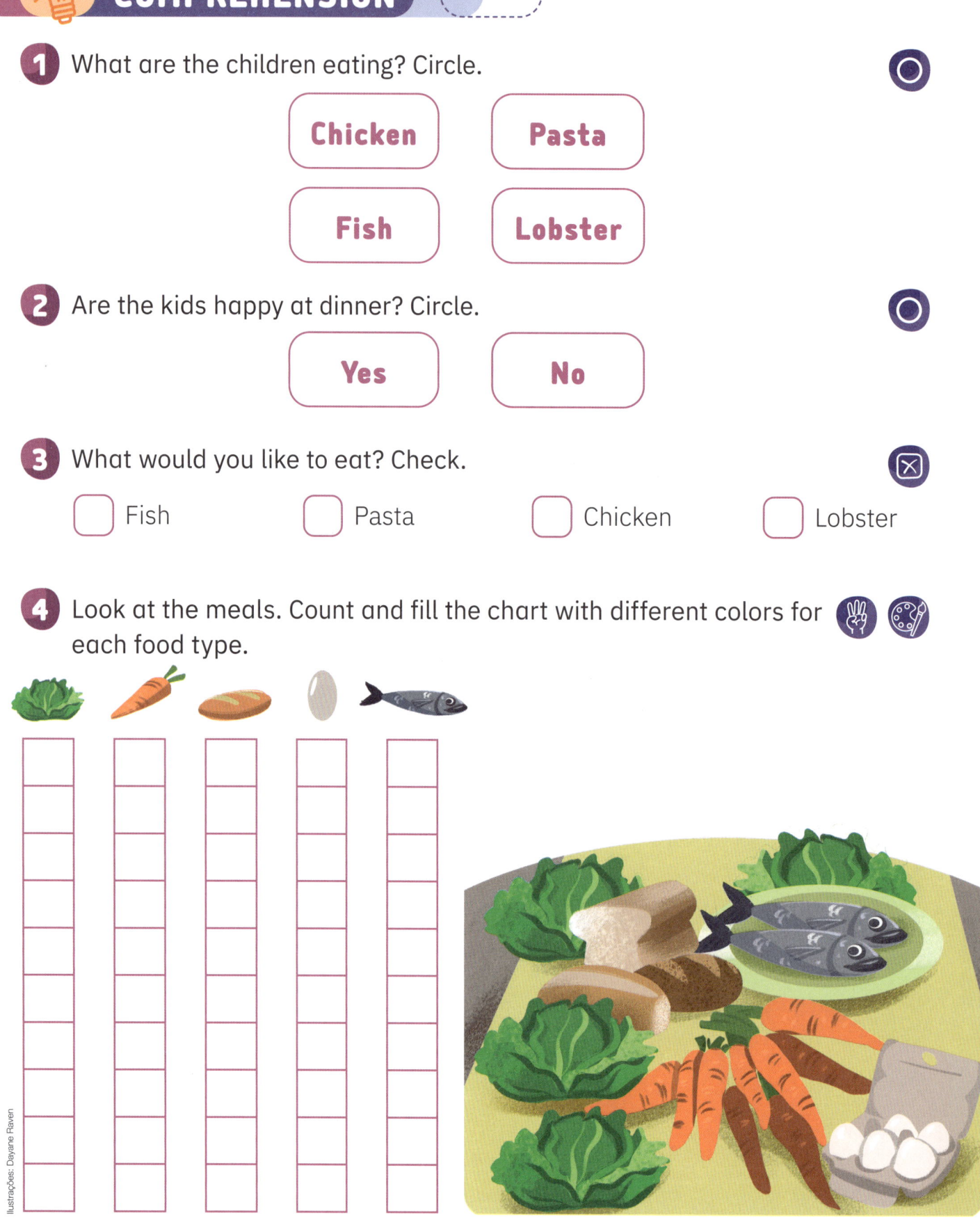

1 What are the children eating? Circle.

- Chicken
- Pasta
- Fish
- Lobster

2 Are the kids happy at dinner? Circle.

- Yes
- No

3 What would you like to eat? Check.

- ☐ Fish
- ☐ Pasta
- ☐ Chicken
- ☐ Lobster

4 Look at the meals. Count and fill the chart with different colors for each food type.

LET'S PLAY

1 Name the foods and drinks using the words from the box.

Juice * Carrot * Lettuce * Meat * Tomato * Potato
Egg * Pasta * Rice * Bread * Water * Beans

a)

b)

c)

d)

e)

f)

g)

h)

i)

j)

k)

l)

SIXTY-THREE 63

2 Read and draw.

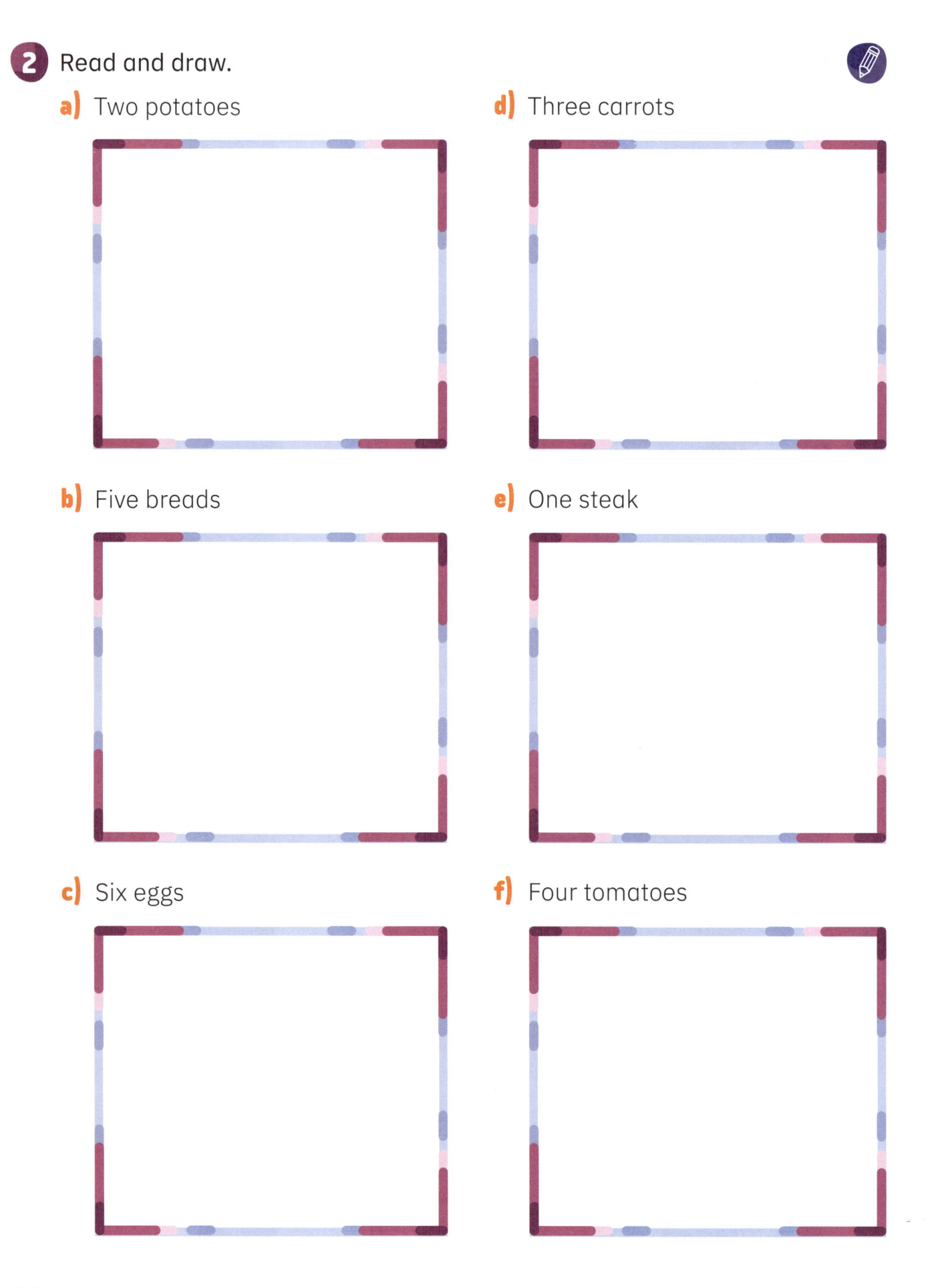

a) Two potatoes

b) Five breads

c) Six eggs

d) Three carrots

e) One steak

f) Four tomatoes

LET'S LISTEN

1 What do they want to buy? Listen and circle the item that is not mentioned. Then write the corresponding word.

a)

b)

c)

d)

e)

LET'S PLAY

1 Find and mark 10 differences between the pictures below.

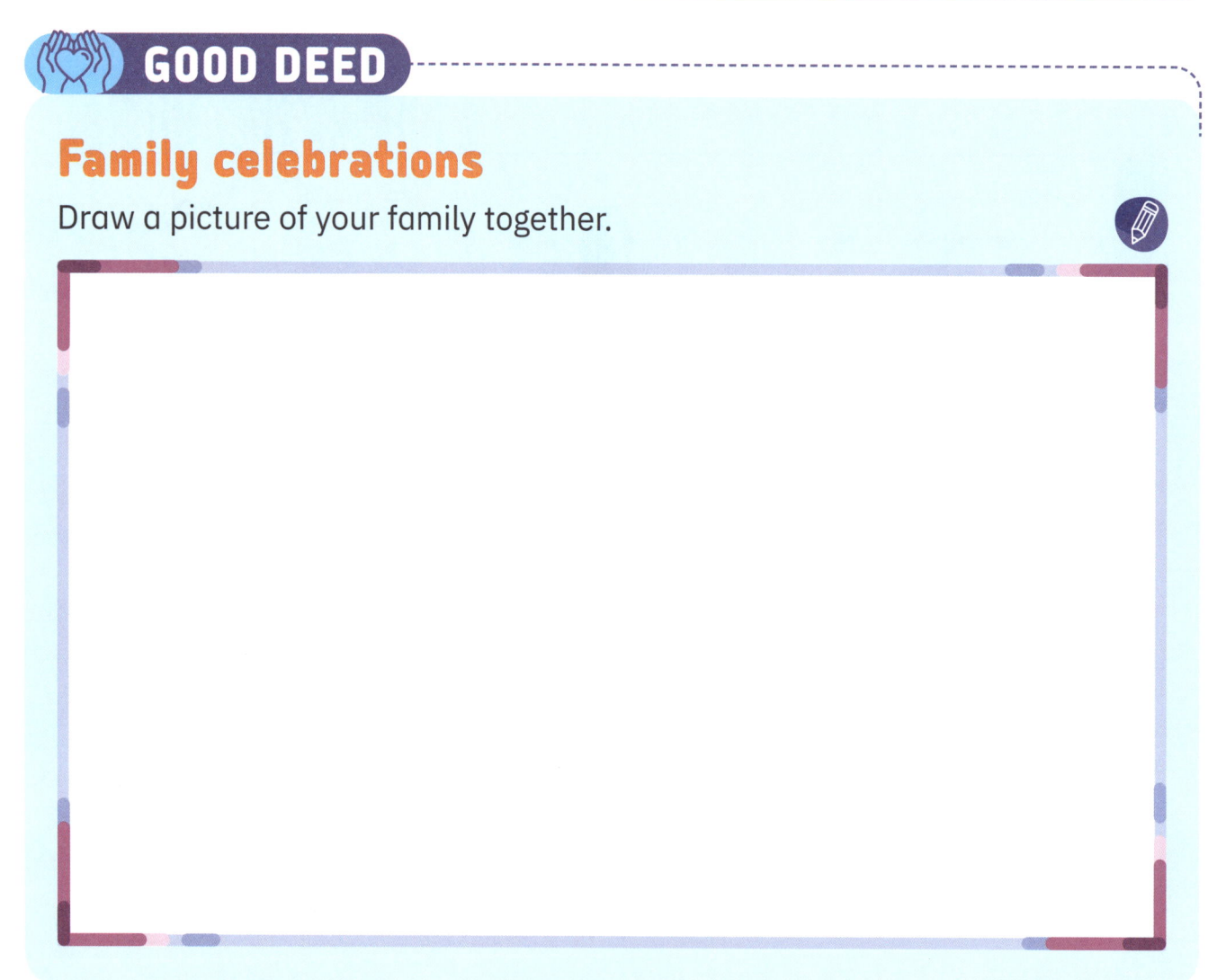

GOOD DEED

Family celebrations

Draw a picture of your family together.

LET'S LISTEN

1 Listen and complete the sentences. Then paste the stickers in the correct place.

a) What's this?

It's a _____.

b) What's this?

It's a bottle of _____.

c) What's this?

It's some _____.

d) What's this?

It's some _____.

SIXTY-SEVEN **67**

I am the baker man

I am the baker man,
I come from far away,
And I can **bake**.
What can you bake?
I can bake **biscuits**!
Crunchy, crunchy, crunchy, crunch,
Crunchy crunch, crunchy crunch!
[...] What can you bake?
I can bake cakes!
Yummy, yummy, yummy, yum,
Yummy, yummy, yum!
[...] What can you bake?
I can bake **cookies**!
Chewy, chewy, chewy, **chew**,
Chewy, chewy, chew!

Nursery rhyme.

LET'S SING!

VOCABULARY

Bake (to bake): assar.
Biscuit(s): biscoito(s).
Chew (to chew): mastigar.
Cookie(s): biscoito(s) redondo(s).
Crunchy: crocante.
Yummy: gostoso.

DIGITAL PLAY

The most popular 4th of July foods

Look at these meals and answer.

Potato salad

Grilled corn

Baked beans

Red, white & blue fruit pizza

Deviled eggs

Smoked ribs

Macaroni salad

Buffalo chicken dip

Smoked brisket

Coleslaw

Ranking available at: Ben Treanor. The most popular July 4th food in every state. *time2play*, [USA], 2023. Accessed on: https://time2play.com/blog/most-popular-july-fourth-food/. Nov. 11, 2023.

Which of these meals would you like to try?

ENGLISH AROUND THE WORLD

Here's how these countries celebrate the Independence Day

Look at the pictures. Then use the words from the box to name each country.

Mexico * Republic of Ghana * Brazil

LET'S PLAY

1 Color the chef and answer.

What is celebrated on October 20?

_____

2 Look at the pictures and complete the words.

a) __ ppl __

b) ch __ rr __ __ s

c) __ r __ ng __

d) l __ m __ n

e) b __ n __ n __

f) gr __ p __ s

g) p __ __ ch

h) p __ __ r

AFTER THIS UNIT I CAN

Identify numbers and quantities.

Identify different kinds of food.

Learn about the typical dishes served on the 4th of July.

Place food orders in formal situations (restaurants, snack bars, cafeterias etc.)

Establish dialogues during playful activities.

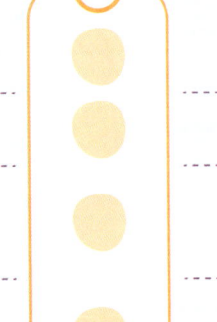

UNIT 6
THE LITTLE FARM

Children, today we will read a story about Mr. Andrew's little farm!

Mr. Andrew has a little farm. He spends a lot of time taking care of it. In the morning, he gets up early and feeds the cows, the chickens, and the pigs.

VOCABULARY

Chicken(s): galinha(s).
Cow(s): vaca(s).
Early: cedo.
Feeds (to feed): alimenta (alimentar).
Gets up (to get up): levanta-se (levantar-se).

In the morning: de/pela manhã.
Little farm: sítio.
Pig(s): porco(s).
Spends (to spend): passa (passar).
Taking care of (to take care of): cuidando de/a/o (cuidar de/a/o).

SEVENTY-THREE 73

COMPREHENSION

1 Where are the children?

☐ In a classroom.

☐ In a barn.

2 What is the story about?

☐ Mr. Andrew and his vegetable garden.

☐ Mr. Andrew and his little farm.

3 Which animals does Mr. Andrew feed on his little farm? Circle them.

sheep

horse

duck

pig

chicken

cow

LET'S LISTEN

1 Now let's listen to what Mr. Andrew does in the afternoon and in the evening. Answer the questions.

a) What does Mr. Andrew do in the afternoon?

☐ He reads.

☐ He takes care of the kitchen and the garden.

b) Which vegetables are there in the vegetable garden? Circle them.

c) What does Mr. Andrew do in the evening?

☐ He reads.

☐ He takes care of the vegetable garden.

d) What does Mr. Andrew like to read?

☐ The news.

☐ Literary fiction books.

ABC GRAMMAR POINT

Question words

What ⟶ O quê?
When ⟶ Quando?
Where ⟶ Onde?/Aonde?

Observe:

A Little Farm Party

April 1st

3:00 o'clock

At St. Thomas School

A Little Farm Party ⟶ What?
April 1st
3:00 o'clock ⟶ When?
At St. Thomas School ⟶ Where?

LET'S PLAY

1 Match each picture to the corresponding word.

- bee
- barn
- horse
- sheep
- cow
- chicken
- pig
- farmer
- dog
- duck

2 Connect the dots and color the animals.

GOOD DEED

Save the bees! Be Kind!

Write the words to save the bees.

Bee KiND

_____

_____

_____

_____

78 SEVENTY-EIGHT

3 Match each animal to its name.

a) Cow

b) Chicken

c) Pig

d) Horse

e) Bird

f) Dog

LET'S LISTEN

1 Listen to the audio. Count and circle the number of farm animals mentioned. Then color them.

LET'S PLAY

1 Find and circle seven differences between the pictures.

LET'S SING!

Mr. Andrew had a little farm

Mr. Andrew had a **little farm**
Ee i ee i o
And on his farm he had **some cows**
Ee i ee i o
With a moo-moo **here**
And a moo-moo **there**
Here a moo, there a moo
Everywhere a moo-moo
Mr. Andrew had a little farm
Ee i ee i o
Mr. Andrew had a little farm
Ee i ee i o
And on his farm he had some **chicks**
Ee i ee i o

With a cluck-cluck here
And a cluck-cluck there
Here a cluck, there a cluck
Everywhere a cluck-cluck
Mr. Andrew had a little farm
Ee i ee i o

Mr. Andrew had a little farm
Ee i ee i o
And on his farm he had some dogs
Ee i ee i o
With a woof-woof here
And a woof-woof there
Here a woof, there a woof
Everywhere a woof-woof
Mr. Andrew had a little farm
Ee i ee i o
Mr. Andrew had a little farm
Ee i ee i o
And on his farm he had a horse
Ee i ee i o
With a neh neh here
And a neh neh there
Here a neh, there a neh
Everywhere a neh neh
Mr. Andrew had a little farm
Ee i ee i o [...]

Popular song. Adapted.

VOCABULARY

Chick(s): pintinho(s).
Cow(s): vaca(s).
Here: aqui.
Little farm: sítio.
Some: alguns/algumas.
There: lá.

DIGITAL PLAY

Curiosities about bees

Paste the stickers. Then, connect the words to the images.

bee

hive

flower

honey

ENGLISH AROUND THE WORLD

Why are bees dying all over the world?

Plant and save bees!

Color the bee.

Calendula

Lavender

Geranium

Thyme

Primula

Sunflower

Salvia

LET'S PLAY

1 Read the comic strip below and interpret it.

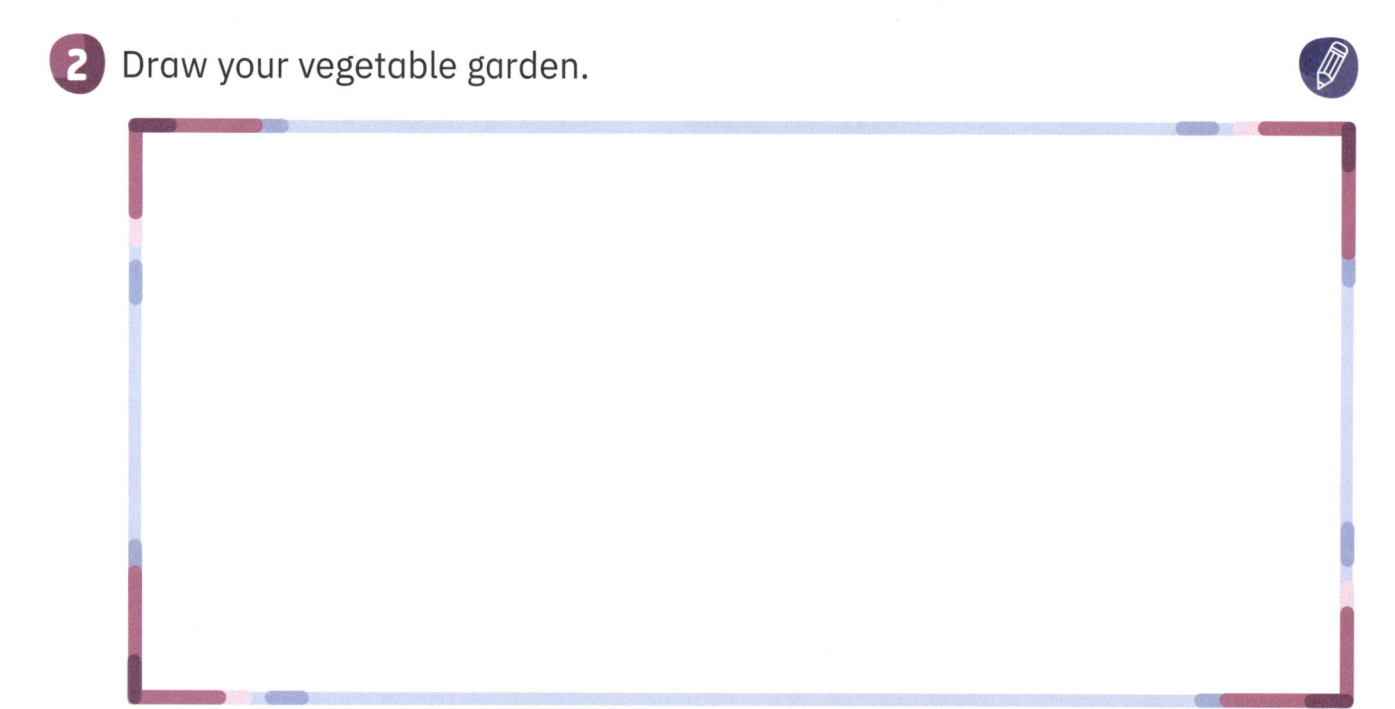

> WHAT ARE DOING WITH THAT MANURE?
>
> PUTTING IT ON THE STRAWBERRIES
>
> WE PUT CREAM ON OURS!

Mike Flanagan/Cartoonstock.com

2 Draw your vegetable garden.

AFTER THIS UNIT I CAN

Identify and use interrogative words.

Identify the names of little farm animals.

Understand the importance of the little farm and country life.

86 EIGHTY-SIX

UNIT 7
AT THE SHOP

T-shirt • Sweater • Socks • Cap
Pants • Dress • Shorts • Pajamas

Hi, **kids**! How can I help you?

I **need** a **T-shirt**!

I **want** a **cap**!

I want a **dress**.

I'm **looking for** a **pair of** shorts.

VOCABULARY

Cap: boné.
Dress: vestido.
How can I help you?: Como posso ajudá-las?
Kids: crianças.
Looking for (to look for): procurando (procurar).

Need (to need): preciso (precisar).
Pair of: par de.
T-shirt: camiseta.
Want (to want): quero (querer).

EIGHTY-SEVEN **87**

COMPREHENSION

1 Where are the children?

☐ In a clothing store.   ☐ In a bookstore.

2 Who wants each item? Color them according to the caption.

- 🟠 Diana
- 🔵 Bill
- 🟡 Laura
- 🟢 Gerry

Cap

Dress

Shorts

T-shirt

LET'S PLAY

1 What are they? Write.

> pants * T-shirt * skirt * sneakers * dress
> shorts * sandals * socks * pajamas * cap

a) _____

b) _____

c) _____

d) _____

e) _____

f) _____

g) _____

h) _____

i) _____

j) _____

EIGHTY-NINE

LET'S LISTEN

1 Listen and color the pictures.

2 How many T-shirts and caps does he have in his closet? Check.

- ☐ Two T-shirts and four caps.
- ☐ Two T-shirts and two caps.
- ☐ Three T-shirts and two caps.

GRAMMAR POINT

Question words

Where ⟶ Aonde? / Onde?
Who ⟶ Quem?

LET'S PLAY

1 Check the appropriate question.

a)  ☐ Where is he?   ☐ Who is he?

b)  ☐ Where is she?   ☐ Who is she?

c)  ☐ Where is he?   ☐ Who is he?

d)  ☐ Where is she?   ☐ Who is she?

GOOD DEED

Personal care of clothes and accessories

Keep each item in the appropriate place. Match the objects.

Drawer

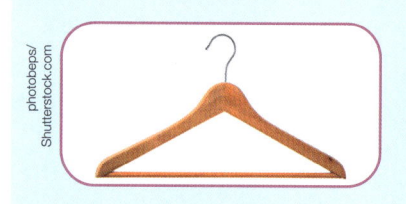

Hanger

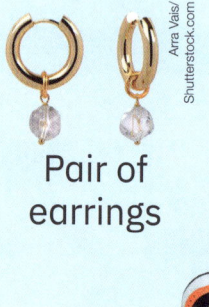

Rack

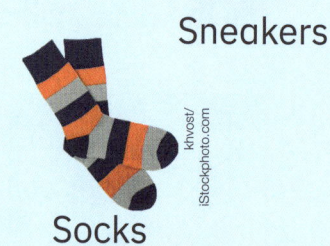

Jewelry case

Dress

Pair of earrings

Sneakers

Socks

T-shirt

ENGLISH AROUND THE WORLD

Winter clothes

Do you wear these clothes when it's cold?

DIGITAL PLAY

Who is wearing...? Where are they?

LET'S SING!

Getting dressed

I'm **getting dressed** myself,
I'm getting dressed myself.
Hi-ho, I'm **growing**-o,
I'm getting dressed myself.
I'm **putting on** my shirt,
I'm putting on my shirt.
Hi-ho, I'm growing-o,
I'm putting on my shirt.
I'm putting on my pants.
I'm putting on my pants.
Hi-ho, I'm growing-o,
I'm putting on my pants.

I'm putting on my socks.
I'm putting on my socks.
Hi-ho, I'm growing-o,
I'm putting on my socks.
I'm putting on my shoes.
I'm putting on my shoes.
Hi-ho, I'm growing-o,
I'm putting on my shoes.
Now look what I have done,
Now look what I have done.
Hi-ho, I'm growing-o,
Now look what I have done.
    Nursery rhyme. Adapted.

VOCABULARY

Getting dressed (To get dressed): me vestindo (se vestir).
Growing (to grow): crescendo (crescer).
Putting on (to put on): colocando/vestindo, (colocar, vestir).

LET'S PLAY

1 Let's play a dressing game! Use stickers and dress the kids.

Check the items you used:

- ☐ dress
- ☐ skirt
- ☐ glasses
- ☐ cap
- ☐ sandals
- ☐ earrings
- ☐ watch
- ☐ socks
- ☐ sneakers
- ☐ shorts
- ☐ T-shirt
- ☐ pants
- ☐ shoes
- ☐ pajamas

AFTER THIS UNIT I CAN

- Greet and respond to others.
- Identify clothing items and accessories.
- Distinguish and use some question words.
- Establish dialogues in playful activities.

UNIT 8
MY CITY

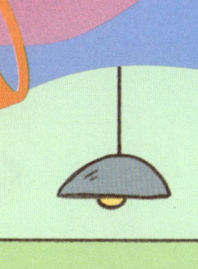

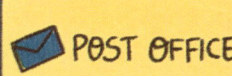

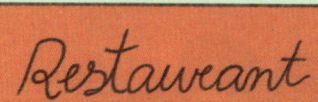

Where do we need to go today, mom?

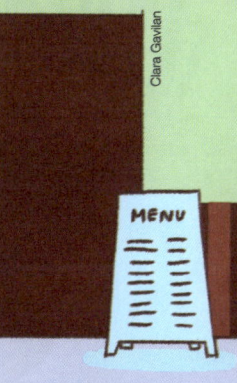

We **need** to go to the **supermarket to buy** some food. After that, we need **to go** to the **post office to post** some letters, and then to the **drugstore** to buy some **medicine**.

Then, we can finally **have lunch** at the **restaurant**.

VOCABULARY

Drugstore: farmácia.
Have lunch: almoçar.
Medicine: remédio.
Need (to need): precisamos (precisar).
Post office: agência de correios.

Restaurant: restaurante.
Supermarket: supermercado.
To buy: comprar.
To go: ir.
To post: postar, enviar.
Where: onde, aonde.

NINETY-SEVEN 97

COMPREHENSION

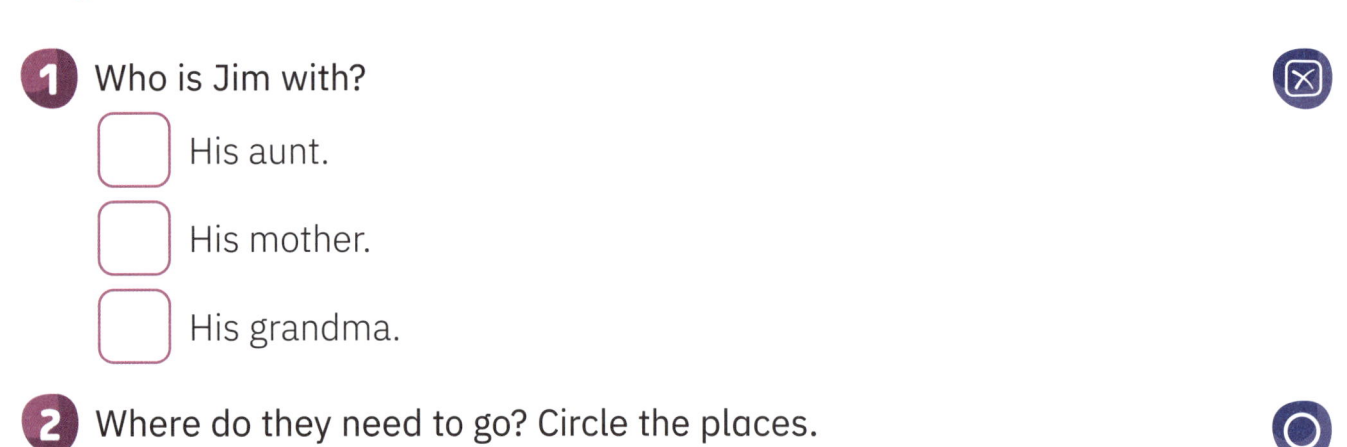

1 Who is Jim with?
- ☐ His aunt.
- ☐ His mother.
- ☐ His grandma.

2 Where do they need to go? Circle the places.

3 What do they need to do in each place?

a) At the supermarket
- ☐ To buy food.
- ☐ To buy some medicine.

c) At the drugstore
- ☐ To buy food.
- ☐ To buy some medicine.

b) At the post office
- ☐ To post some letters.
- ☐ To have lunch.

d) At the restaurant
- ☐ To post some letters.
- ☐ To have lunch.

LET'S PLAY

1 Trace the words and match them to the corresponding places.

a) DRUGSTORE

b) RESTAURANT

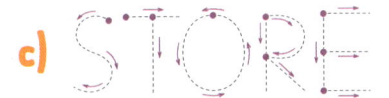

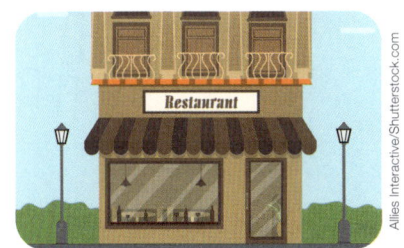

c) STORE

d) BANK

e) POLICE STATION

f) SUPERMARKET

LET'S LISTEN

1 Listen to the sentences. Then read and color the places.

- It is a green park.
- It is a yellow bank.
- It is an orange post office.
- It is a brown supermarket.
- It is a blue police station.
- It is a pink drugstore.
- It is a red school.
- It is a grey hospital.

LET'S PLAY

1 Let's play bingo!

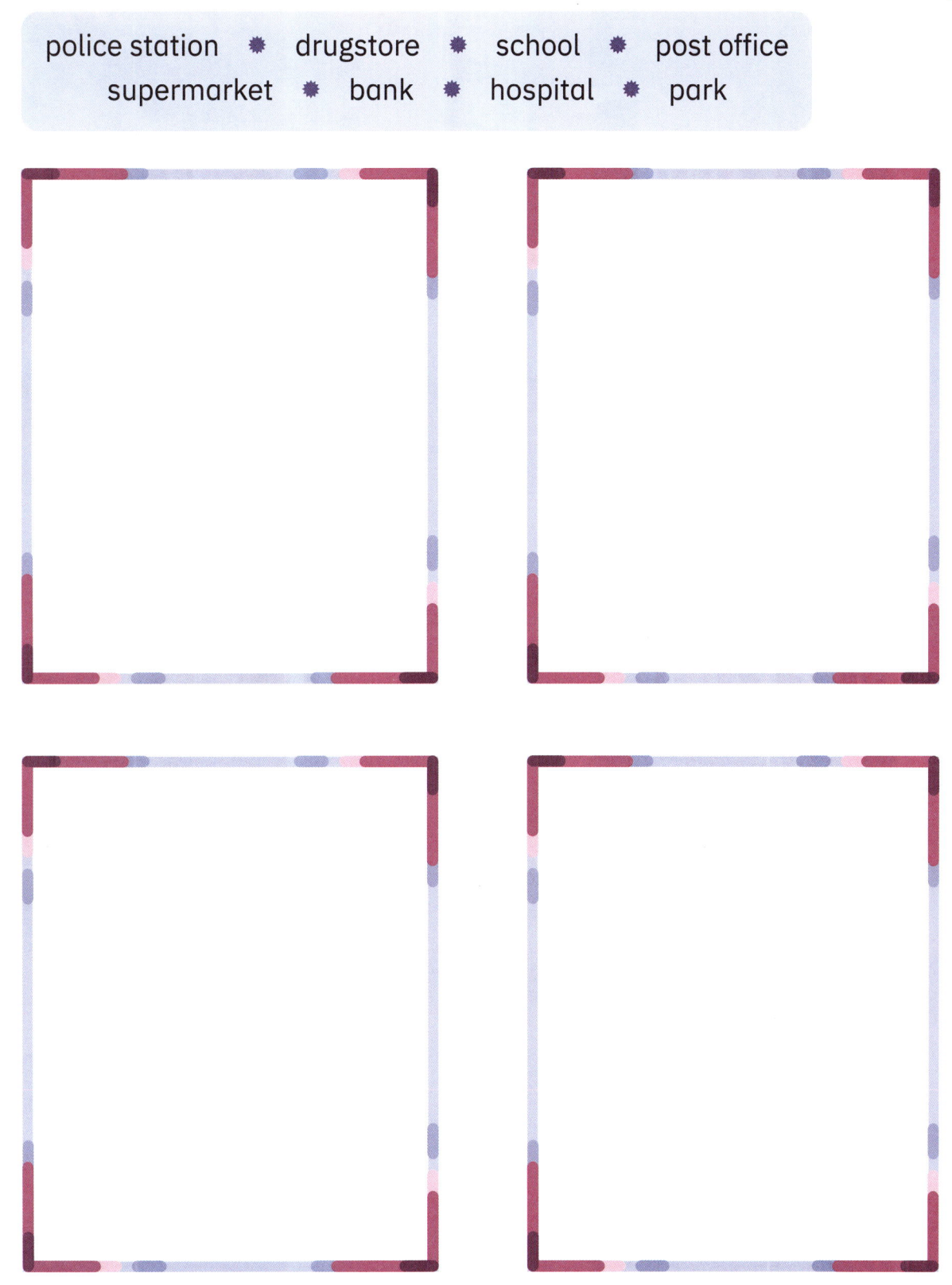

police station • drugstore • school • post office
supermarket • bank • hospital • park

LET'S LISTEN

1 Listen and paste the correct sticker.

a)

c)

b)

d)

LET'S PLAY

1 Match the things you have in your city.

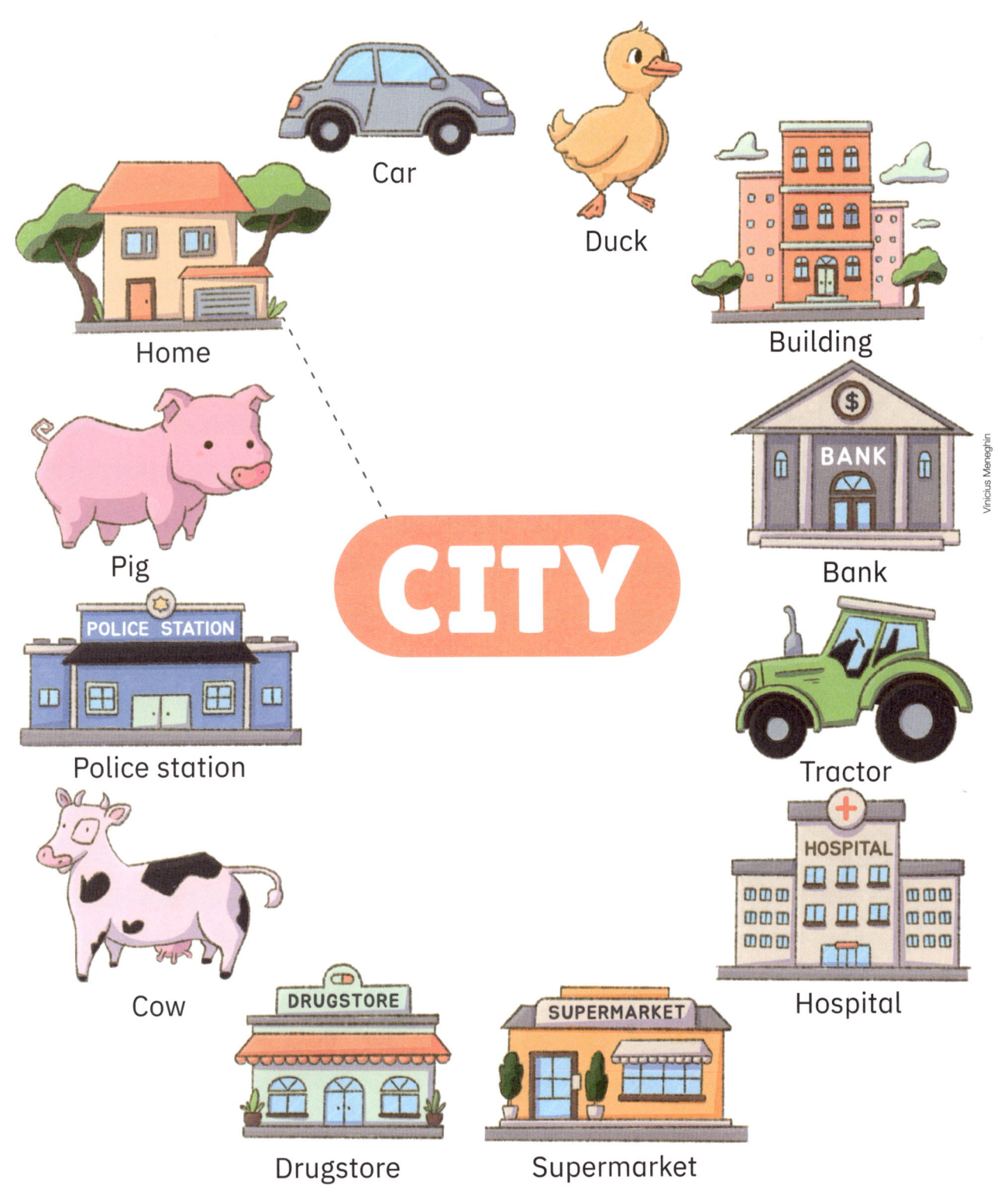

Car

Duck

Building

Home

Bank

Pig

Tractor

Police station

Hospital

Cow

Drugstore   Supermarket

CITY

LET'S SING!

This is the key to the city

This is the **key** to the city.
In that **city** there is a **street**.
On that street there is a **house**.
In that house there is a **room**.
In that room there is a **bed**.
On that bed there is a **basket**.
In that basket there are some flowers.
Flowers in the basket,
Basket on the bed,
Bed in the room,
Room in the house,
House on the street,
And street in the city –
This is the key to the city.

Traditional nursery rhyme. Adapted.

VOCABULARY

Basket: cesta.
Bed: cama.
City: cidade.
House: casa.
Key: chave.
Room: quarto, cômodo.
Street: rua.

GOOD DEED

We must take care of our city!

1 Let's make a model of a city.

2 Draw the city of your dreams.

DIGITAL PLAY

Las Vegas, the brightest city in the world

ENGLISH AROUND THE WORLD

Sphere is a next-generation entertainment medium that is redefining the future.

What kind of technology do you like? What's the name of the new technology attraction in Las Vegas?

AFTER THIS UNIT I CAN

- Observe and understand a city map to identify places.
- Identify some places in the city.
- Establish dialogues in playful activities.

REVIEW

Unit 1

1 Solve the wordsearch. Then, trace the words.

pencil • eraser • pencil sharpener
pen • notebook • book

I	E	E	S	N	O	T	E	B	O	O	K	T	Q	T
H	Y	T	V	R	S	A	S	W	T	R	P	E	I	E
U	T	S	E	P	H	T	S	A	E	R	E	F	A	D
N	H	S	E	E	O	S	T	S	N	O	N	O	Y	V
B	T	A	A	N	U	A	Q	N	D	A	C	S	C	R
T	A	R	F	E	A	E	N	F	N	R	I	K	H	I
O	G	N	A	L	D	W	I	A	S	P	L	A	W	Q
P	E	N	C	I	L	S	H	A	R	P	E	N	E	R
S	S	A	H	O	P	E	R	A	S	E	R	B	O	I
F	B	O	O	K	E	S	N	X	Y	N	E	R	P	E

a) pencil

b) eraser

c) pencil sharpener

d) pen

e) notebook

f) book

2 Color the letters of your favorite color. Then, write the name of the color.

A B C D E F G H I J
K L M N O P Q
R S T U V W X Y Z

My favorite color is _____.

3 How many school objetcs are there on the table? Count and write.

a) _____ notebook.

b) _____ book.

c) _____ colored pens.

d) _____ colored pencils.

e) _____ erasers.

f) _____ pencil case.

4 Circle the classroom items.

bed

bookshelf

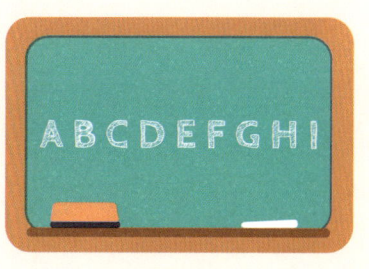

board

desk

wastebasket

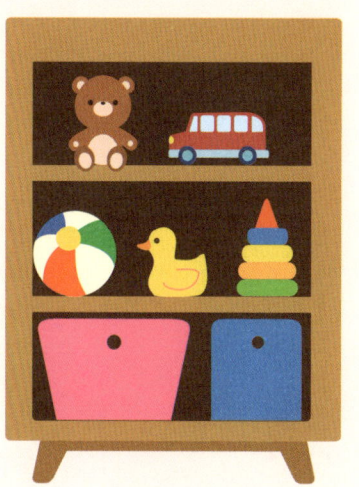

shelf

sofa

sink

fan

chair

window

lamp

ONE HUNDRED NINE **109**

5 Find and circle the name of the colors in the wordsearch.

> black ✸ blue ✸ brown ✸ green
> orange ✸ pink ✸ red ✸ yellow
> white ✸ gray ✸ purple

C	R	E	D	X	T	Y	T	Y	Z	Y	K
B	M	G	E	S	N	A	B	A	I	I	A
P	T	T	Y	O	O	E	P	I	N	K	A
R	G	R	E	E	N	H	U	S	S	O	I
I	T	A	L	S	L	E	R	B	B	P	B
E	I	L	L	F	V	E	P	L	N	O	R
N	C	G	O	H	T	N	L	A	S	R	O
A	B	R	W	H	I	T	E	C	N	A	W
I	O	A	E	A	P	I	T	K	O	N	N
O	N	Y	A	O	E	O	E	A	Y	G	B
H	S	E	O	A	N	S	B	L	U	E	M
H	L	H	S	W	T	Y	O	A	Y	N	C

6 Draw and name a school item. Then, paint it with your favorite color.

110 ONE HUNDRED TEN

Unit 2

1 Draw your family.

Now, complete the sentences.

My name is _____.

My mother's name is _____.

My father's name is _____.

2 Put the words from the box in the correct columns.

> aunt * grandmother * Thursday * Friday *
> brother * Monday * Tuesday * grandfather *
> cousin * mother * uncle * sister * father *
> Saturday * Wednesday * Sunday

Days of the week	Family members

3 Answer the questions.

a) What is your favorite day of the week?
_____

b) What do you like to do on this day?
_____

Unit 3

1 Look at the picture and complete the text with the words.

Zoo ✸ wild

These animals live in the _____.
But we can see them and learn to preserve them at the
_____.

Unit 4

1 Complete the calendar with the missing months.

 January	 February	 _____	 April
 _____	 June	 _____	 August
 September	 _____	 November	 _____

Unit 5

1 Match each food item to its corresponding word.

a) Orange

b) Bread

c) Banana

d) Butter

e) Milk

f) Cake

g) Egg

h) Apple

Unit 6

1 Check only on the animals that live on the farm.

- ☐ Elephant.
- ☐ Pig.
- ☐ Alligator.
- ☐ Chicken.
- ☐ Lion.
- ☐ Horse.
- ☐ Zebra.
- ☐ Cow.
- ☐ Giraffe.

2 Look at the animals and match the corresponding shadow.

Unit 7

1 Find and color the clothing items.

> one T-shirt • one pair of pants • three shoes
> five caps • four skirts • one shirt

Unit 8

1 What is it? Solve and match with the corresponding image.

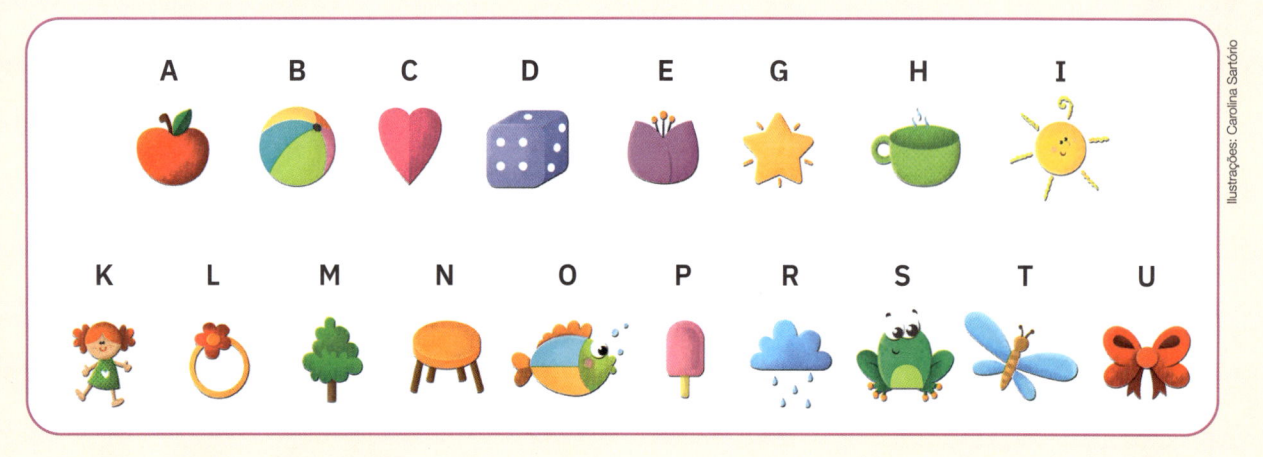

A	B	C	D	E	G	H	I
K	L	M	N	O	P	R	S	T	U

a)
b)
c)
d)

2 Look at the pictures and circle one word to name it.

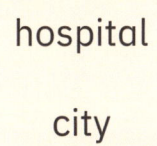

hospital

city

house

hospital

house

park

bank

park

school

house

hospital

school

library

park

school

ONE HUNDRED NINETEEN 119

PICTURE DICTIONARY

A

Alligator

Basket

Birthday party

Aunt

Beans

Butter

C

Bed

Cafeteria

B

Bank

Bird

Cake

120 ONE HUNDRED TWENTY

Calendar

Candies

Cap

Carrot

Chick

Chicken

Classroom

Coffee

Corn

Court

Cousin

Cow

D

Dad

Dishes

E

Eggs

Father

Dress

Elephant

French fries

Drugstore

F

G

Family

Giraffe

Duck

Graduation party

Hot dog

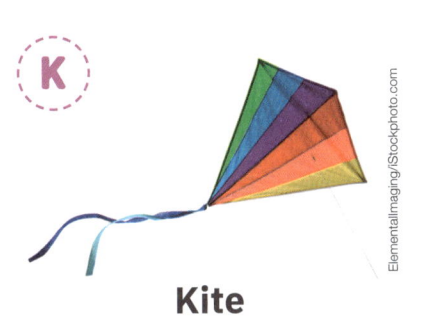

K

Kite

H

Hamburger

I

Ice cream

L

Lemon juice

Lettuce

Hospital

Invitation

House

J

Juice

Library

ONE HUNDRED TWENTY-THREE 123

Little farm

M

Meat

Mom

Monkey

Mother

Notebook

P

Pants

Pasta

Pencil

Pajamas

Pig

Police station

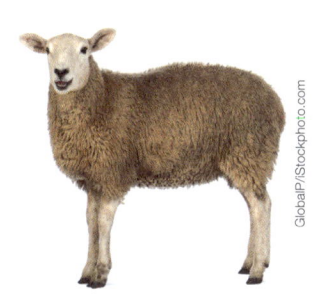

Post office	**Restaurant**	**School**
Potato	**Rice**	**Sheep**
Pumpkin	**Salad**	**Shorts**
R		
Rabbit	**Sandals**	**Sister**
	Sandwich	

Skirt

Sneakers

Socks

Soda

Soup

Steak

Store

Sunglasses

Supermarket

Sweater

Swimming cap

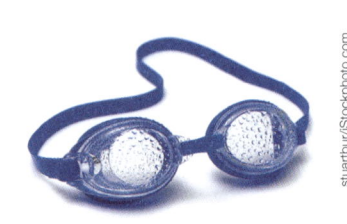

Swimming goggles

T

Tea

Tomato

T-shirt

Turtle

W

Watch

Z

Zebra

U

Uncle

Water

V

Wild animals

Vegetable garden

ONE HUNDRED TWENTY-SEVEN **127**

INDEX

SONGS

UNIT 1	This is the way we laugh and play	27
UNIT 2	Days of the week	36
UNIT 3	The elephant has a great big trunk	46
UNIT 4	Happy birthday!	59
UNIT 5	I am the baker man	68
UNIT 6	Mr. Andrew had a little farm	82
UNIT 7	Getting dressed	94
UNIT 8	This is the key to the city	104

LISTENINGS

UNIT 1
- New classmates — 19
- Today is the first day of school — 21
- Talking about schools — 26

UNIT 2
- Friends and family — 29
- Days of the week — 31
- Jack's family — 37

UNIT 3
- A visit to the zoo — 39
- Wild animals — 43
- Animals and kids — 43

UNIT 4
- The birthday party — 49
- Jim's birthday party — 51
- Days of the month — 54
- Class birthday list — 55

UNIT 5
- Let's cook! — 61
- What do they want to buy? — 65
- What's this? — 67

UNIT 6
- The little farm — 73
- Mr. Andrew's little farm — 75
- Farm animals — 80

UNIT 7
- At the shop — 87
- Bill's clothes colors — 90

UNIT 8
- My city — 97
- Places and colors — 100
- Places — 102

CELEBRATIONS

Easter

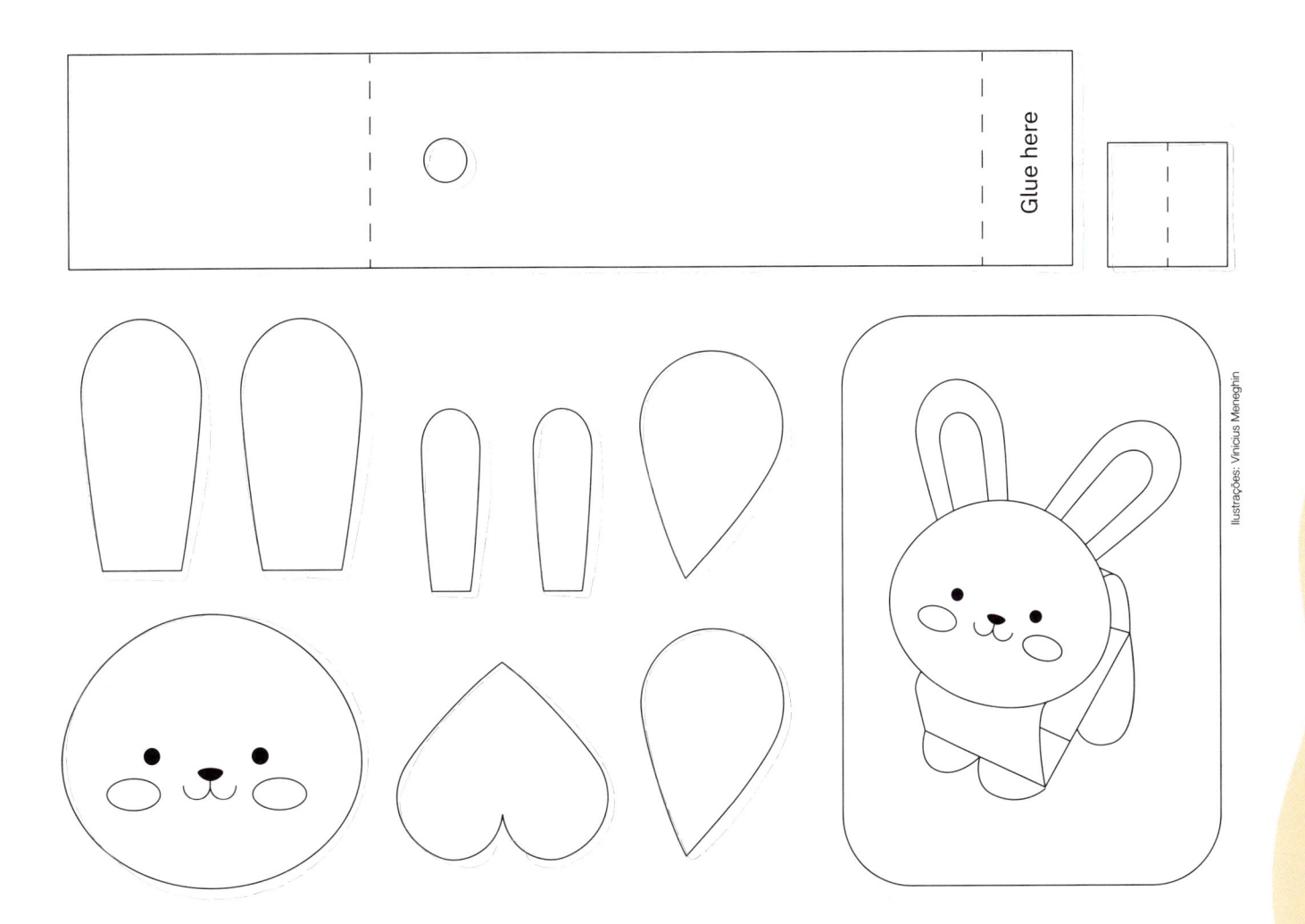

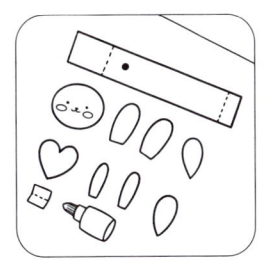

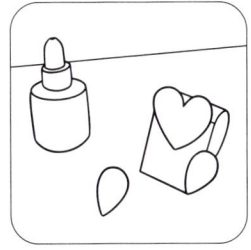

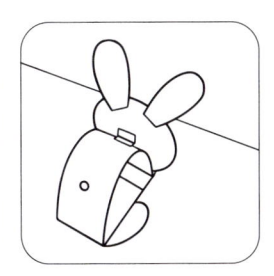

Glue here

Global Recycling Day

Victoria Day

Glue here

Glue here

International Family's Day

I love my family!

International Family's Day

S'mores Day

Graham crackers

Graham crackers

Chocolate

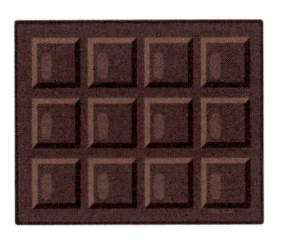

Chocolate

Marshmallow

Marshmallow

Bonfire

Bonfire

S'more

S'more

Christmas

Merry Christmas!

New Year's Eve
Happy New Year!

H A P

P Y N

E W Y

E A R !

STICKERS

Let's start!
Page 16

Unit 1
Page 24

Library

Cafeteria

Classroom

Court

Unit 2

Page 32

Sunday	Thursday	Wednesday
Tuesday	Friday	Saturday

Unit 3

Page 43

Gorilla Camel Giratte Lion

Unit 4

Page 51

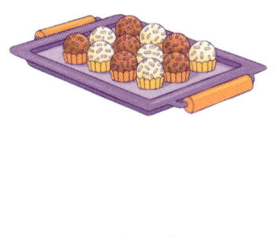

STICKERS

STICKERS

Unit 5
Page 67

Unit 6
Page 84

ONE HUNDRED FORTY-NINE 149

STICKERS

Unit 7
Page 96

Unit 8
Page 102

Supermarket

Post office

Bank

Drugstore

BRINCANDO
COM INGLÊS

WORKBOOK

2

**ENSINO FUNDAMENTAL
ANOS INICIAIS**

**RENATO MENDES CURTO JÚNIOR
ANNA CAROLINA GUIMARÃES
CIBELE MENDES**

Editora do Brasil

CONTENTS

UNIT 1
New classmates — 3

UNIT 2
Friends and family — 4

UNIT 3
A visit to the zoo — 9

UNIT 4
The birthday party — 15

UNIT 5
Let's cook! — 20

UNIT 6
The little farm — 24

UNIT 7
At the shop — 27

UNIT 8
My city — 29

UNIT 1
NEW CLASSMATES

1 Complete the dialogues with the correct subject pronoun and its verb **to be** form.

a) Class, this is Patty.
_____ your new classmate.

b) Patty, this is David.
_____ my friend.

UNIT 2
FRIENDS AND FAMILY

1 Unscramble the letters and find the family members.

a) OMRHTE: _____

b) FETAHR: _____

c) RROTBEH: _____

d) RGRETAHNAFD: _____

e) RGREOHTNAMD: _____

f) EUNCL: _____

g) NAUT: _____

h) CNOUIS: _____

2 Look at the images and write **we are** or **they are**.

a)

_____ a family.

b)

_____ brothers.

3 Write the words below in the right spaces on the family tree.

Mother * Brother * Grandfather
Sister * Grandmother * Father

Me

4 Link the family members in portuguese with their English form.

Primo/prima   * Aunt

Tia   * Uncle

Tio   * Cousin

5 Choose one person and:

* Draw his/her portrait.

* Write which member of your family he/she is:
  This is my _____

UNIT 3
A VISIT TO THE ZOO

1 What wild animal is it? Name them with the words in the box.

> Zebra • Elephant • Giraffe
> Monkey • Alligator • Lion

a) _____

c) _____

e) _____

b) _____

d) _____

f) _____

NINE 9

2 Find the wild animals in the word search.

Zebra

Giraffe

Alligator

Elephant

Monkey

Lion

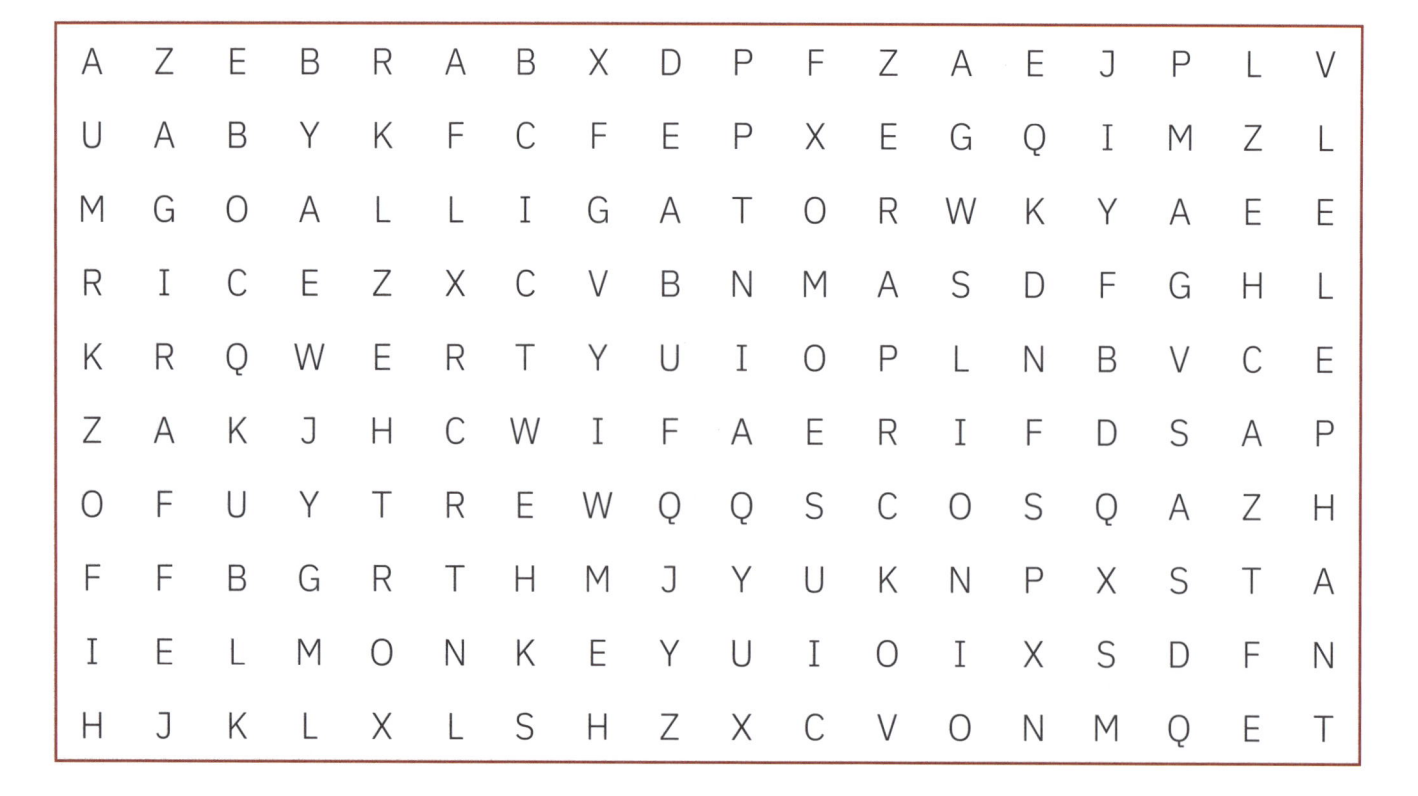

A	Z	E	B	R	A	B	X	D	P	F	Z	A	E	J	P	L	V
U	A	B	Y	K	F	C	F	E	P	X	E	G	Q	I	M	Z	L
M	G	O	A	L	L	I	G	A	T	O	R	W	K	Y	A	E	E
R	I	C	E	Z	X	C	V	B	N	M	A	S	D	F	G	H	L
K	R	Q	W	E	R	T	Y	U	I	O	P	L	N	B	V	C	E
Z	A	K	J	H	C	W	I	F	A	E	R	I	F	D	S	A	P
O	F	U	Y	T	R	E	W	Q	Q	S	C	O	S	Q	A	Z	H
F	F	B	G	R	T	H	M	J	Y	U	K	N	P	X	S	T	A
I	E	L	M	O	N	K	E	Y	U	I	O	I	X	S	D	F	N
H	J	K	L	X	L	S	H	Z	X	C	V	O	N	M	Q	E	T

3 Now, answer:

What is it?

a)

_____

b)

_____

c)

_____

d)

_____

e)

_____

f)

_____

ELEVEN 11

4 Look at the zoo. Write the number of the animals you can find.

How many?

- How many elephants are there? _____
- How many lions are there? _____
- How many zebras are there? _____
- How many giraffes are there? _____
- How many trees are there? _____

5 Complete the alphabet.

a b ◯ d ◯ f ◯ h i j k ◯ m

n ◯ p q r ◯ t u ◯ w x ◯ z

6 What is the first letter of the names of these animals?

1. _____
2. _____
3. _____
4. _____
5. _____

THIRTEEN 13

7 Guessing game: "Where is the animal?" Your teacher will tag you with a picture of an animal. Try to guess which animal it is and where it is from. Remember to listen to the tips from your classmates.

Example
— You jump. You carry your baby in a bag.
— I am a kangaroo.
— Yes!

— Where is your animal from?
— From Australia.
— That's correct!

UNIT 4
THE BIRTHDAY PARTY

1 Look at Sammy's invitation and complete it with the information in the box.

> Sammy's house • Sunday •
> Two o'clock • Anna

YOU ARE INVITED TO MY BIRTHDAY PARTY!

FOR _____

DATE _____

TIME _____

PLACE _____

FIFTEEN 15

2 Read Carol's message to Peter and complete it with **am** or **are**.

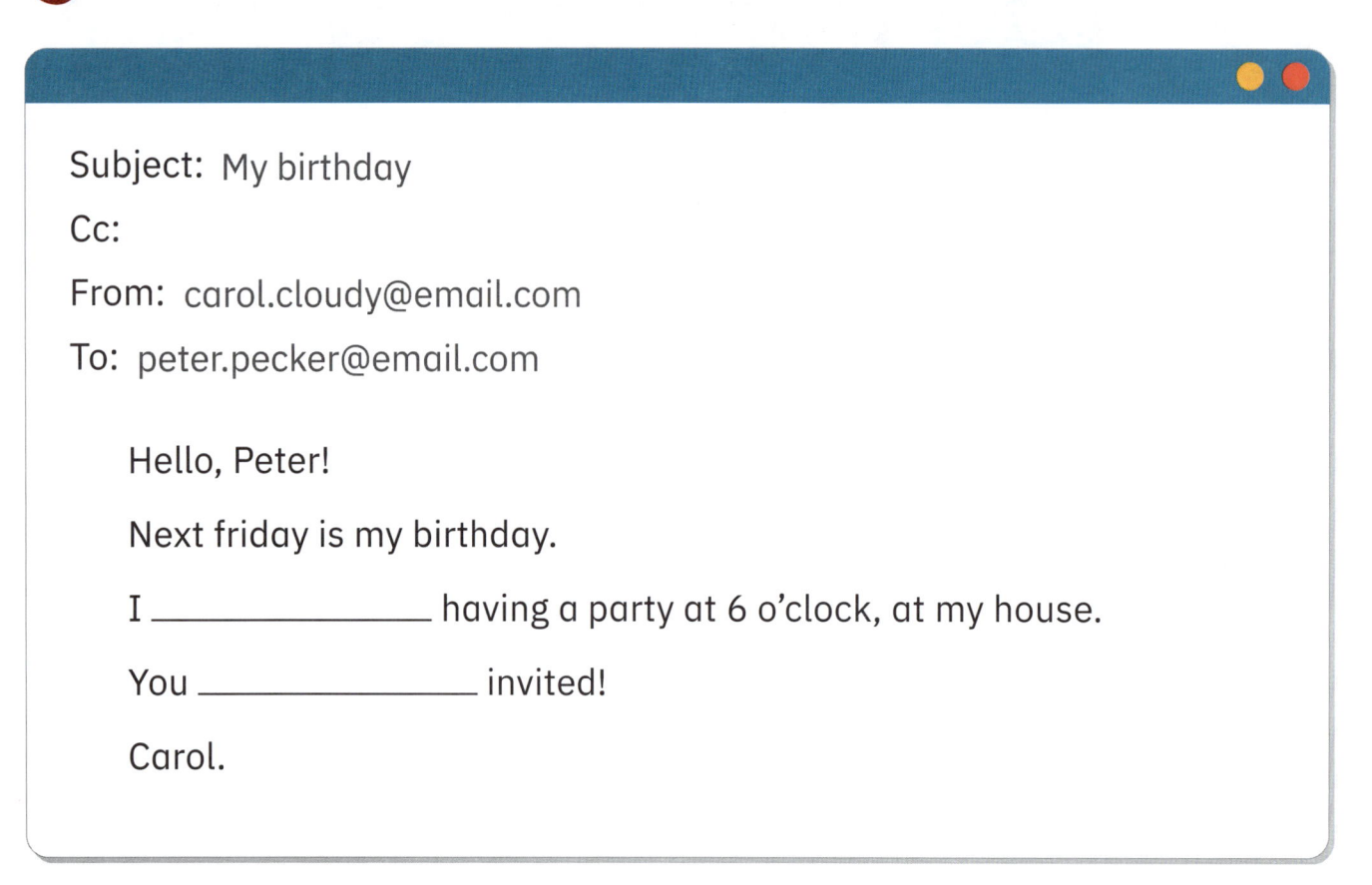

Subject: My birthday
Cc:
From: carol.cloudy@email.com
To: peter.pecker@email.com

Hello, Peter!

Next friday is my birthday.

I _____ having a party at 6 o'clock, at my house.

You _____ invited!

Carol.

* Now, read Peter's response to Carol and complete it with **am** or **are**.

Subject: Re: My birthday
Cc:
From: peter.pecker@email.com
To: carol.cloudy@email.com

Hello, Carol!

Thank you for the invitation!

I _____ going to the party.

Peter.

3 Read this invitation. What is it for?

WHAT?
MY BIRTHDAY PARTY!

WHEN?
JANUARY 16ᵀᴴ

WHERE?
AT MY HOME
(37, HOWARD STREET)

COME AND HAVE SOME FUN!

ALICE

_____
_____
_____

* Look at the birthday party invitation to answer the questions.

   a) Who's having a birthday?
   _____

   b) Where does he/she live?
   _____

4 Complete the invitation with the information in the box.

Next Sunday

A picnic

Municipal park

WHAT?

WHEN?

WHERE?

COME AND HAVE SOME FUN!

5 Mark with an **X** only the birthday party food.

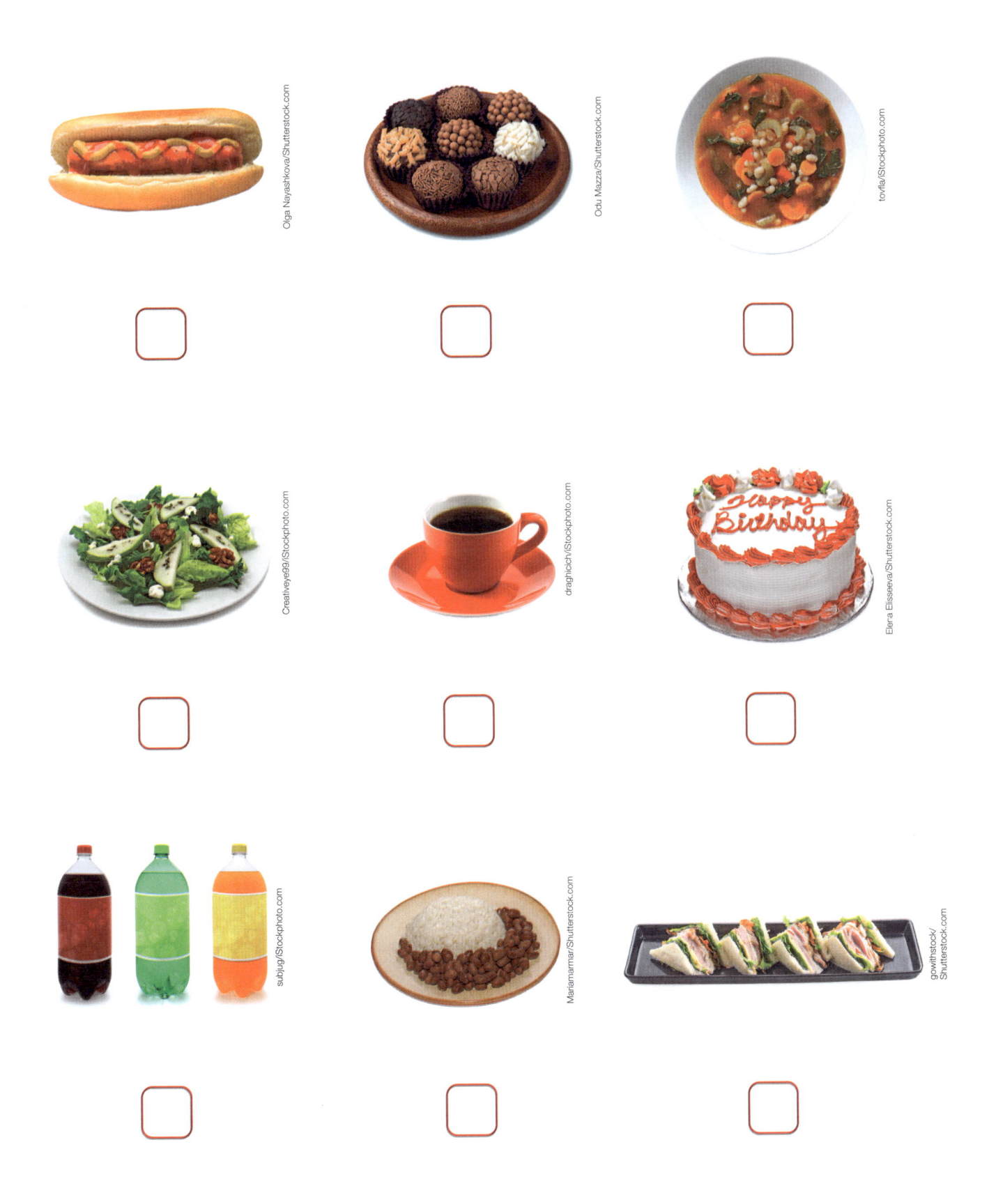

NINETEEN 19

UNIT 5
LET'S COOK!

1 What are they? Choose a word from the box and name the food.

> Juice • Carrot • Lettuce • Meat • Tomato • Potato
> Egg • Pasta • Rice • Bread • Water • Soda

a) _____

b) _____

c) _____

d) _____

e) _____

f) _____

g) _____

h) _____

i) _____

j) _____

k) _____

l) _____

2 Look at the images and complete the sentences. Do as the example.

a) There is an ____onion____, a _____ and an _____.

b) There are two _____, six _____ and five _____.

3 Match the words to the images.

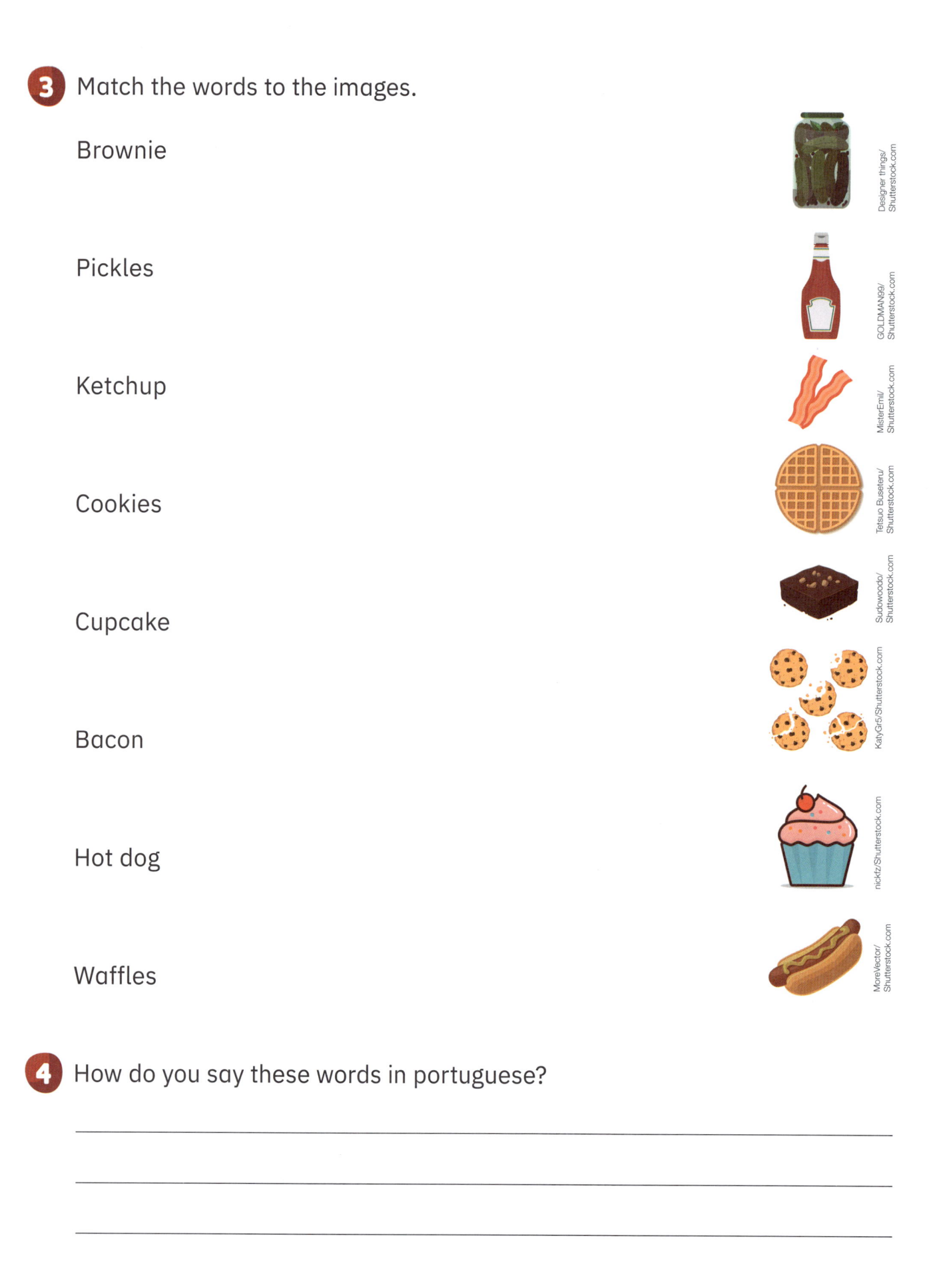

Brownie

Pickles

Ketchup

Cookies

Cupcake

Bacon

Hot dog

Waffles

4 How do you say these words in portuguese?

_____

_____

_____

5 Find seven differences between the two pictures and name all the food you see.

_____

_____

TWENTY-THREE 23

UNIT 6
THE LITTLE FARM

1 Which of these animals are farm animals? Circle them.

* Now write the names of all these farm animals.

_____

_____

_____

2 What do we grow in a kitchen garden?

- ☐ Flowers.
- ☐ Fruits.
- ☐ Vegetables.

3 Color all the vegetables.

Apple

Onion

Strawberry

Beans

Grape

Carrot

Pineapple

Cabbage

Watermelon

Orange

Tomato

Corn

Potato

UNIT 7
AT THE SHOP

1 Circle the clothes that you would buy and complete the lists with the correct clothes for each body part.

Head	Body	Feet
_____	_____	_____
_____	_____	_____
_____	_____	_____
_____	_____	_____

TWENTY-SEVEN 27

2 Name the clothing items correctly.

> Cap * Shorts * Skirt * T-shirt *
> Pants * Sneakers * Socks * Dress *
> Shoes * Sweater * Pajamas * Sandals

a)

b)

c)

d)

e)

f)

g)

h)

i)

j)

k)

l)

UNIT 8
MY CITY

1 Match the places with their names.

a)

b)

c)

d)

e)

- Drugstore

- Supermarket

- Restaurant

- Police station

- Bank

Ilustrações: Luiz Lentini

TWENTY-NINE **29**

2 What places can you identify in the map? Name all of them.

3 Draw what you like most when you are…

a) On the beach…

I like…

b) At the campsite…

I like…

4 Where can you go on holiday? Match the places to the correct pictures.

Beach

Cinema

Zoo

Park

Farm

Campsite

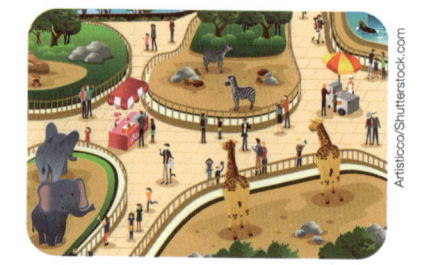

It's my Birthday!

Ilustrações © Ronaldo Barata

© Editora do Brasil S.A., 2024
Todos os direitos reservados

Direção-geral	Paulo Serino de Souza
Direção editorial	Felipe Ramos Poletti
Gerência editorial de produção e design	Ulisses Pires
Supervisão editorial	Carla Felix Lopes e Diego da Mata
Edição	Camile Mendrot | Ab Aeterno
Assistência editorial	Marcos Vasconcelos e Pedro Andrade Bezerra; Enrico Payão | Ab Aeterno
Auxílio editorial	Natalia Soeda
Supervisão de arte	Abdonildo José de Lima Santos
Edição de arte e diagramação	Ana Clara Suzano | Ab Aeterno
Design gráfico	Ariane Adriele O. Costa
Supervisão de revisão	Elaine Cristina da Silva
Revisão	Natasha Greenhouse e Sarah Garnett | Ab Aeterno

1ª edição / 1ª impressão, 2024
Impresso na Hawaii Gráfica e Editora

Editora do Brasil

Avenida das Nações Unidas, 12901
Torre Oeste, 20º andar
São Paulo, SP – CEP: 04578-910
www.editoradobrasil.com.br

abdr
ASSOCIAÇÃO BRASILEIRA DOS DIREITOS REPROGRÁFICOS
Respeite o direito autoral

It's my Birthday!

MARIA CAROLINA RODRIGUES

ILUSTRAÇÕES: RONALDO BARATA

Editora do Brasil

It is almost time...
January, February, March... **April!**
One, two, three, four, five, six, seven, eight, nine, ten... **eleven!**
Monday, Tuesday…
Wednesday!

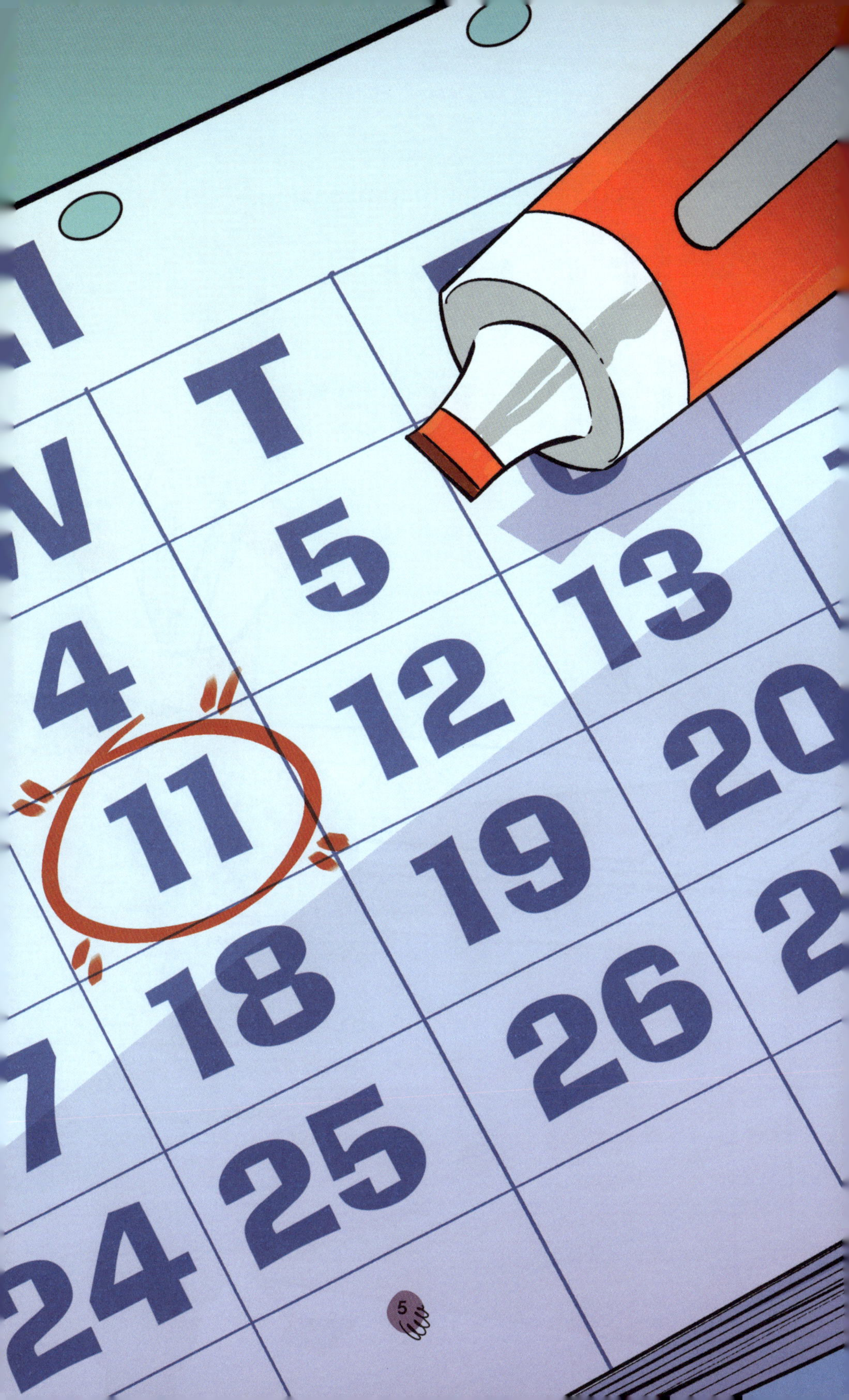
T
5
13
4
12
20
11
19
18
26
7
25
24

Do you know what that means?
It's my birthday!

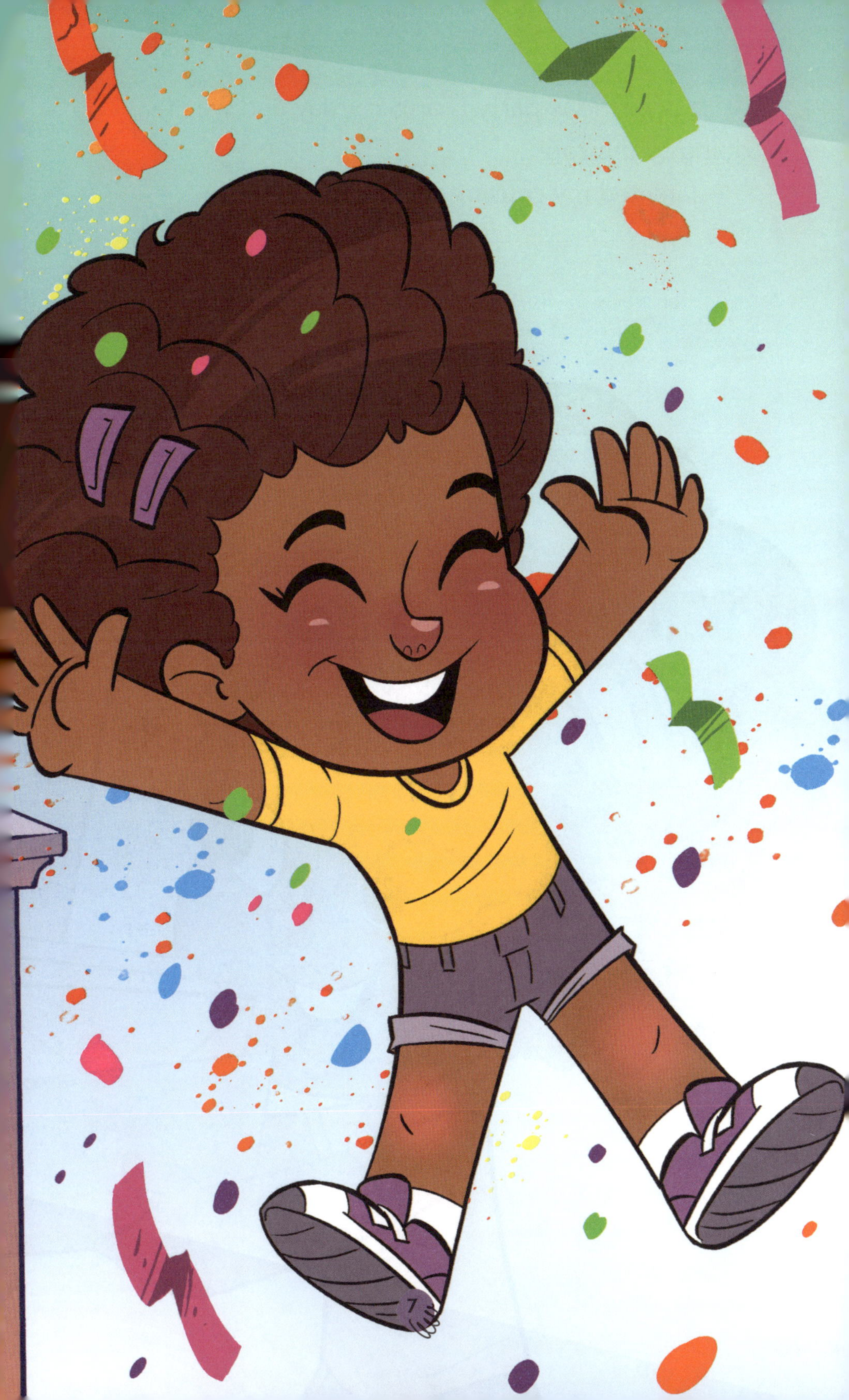

My birthday party is on Saturday and we are going to the zoo!
I invited my cousins and all my friends.

You are invited to my birthday!

We will play and run and jump and laugh.

We will see an alligator and an elephant and a giraffe and a lion and a gorilla!

11

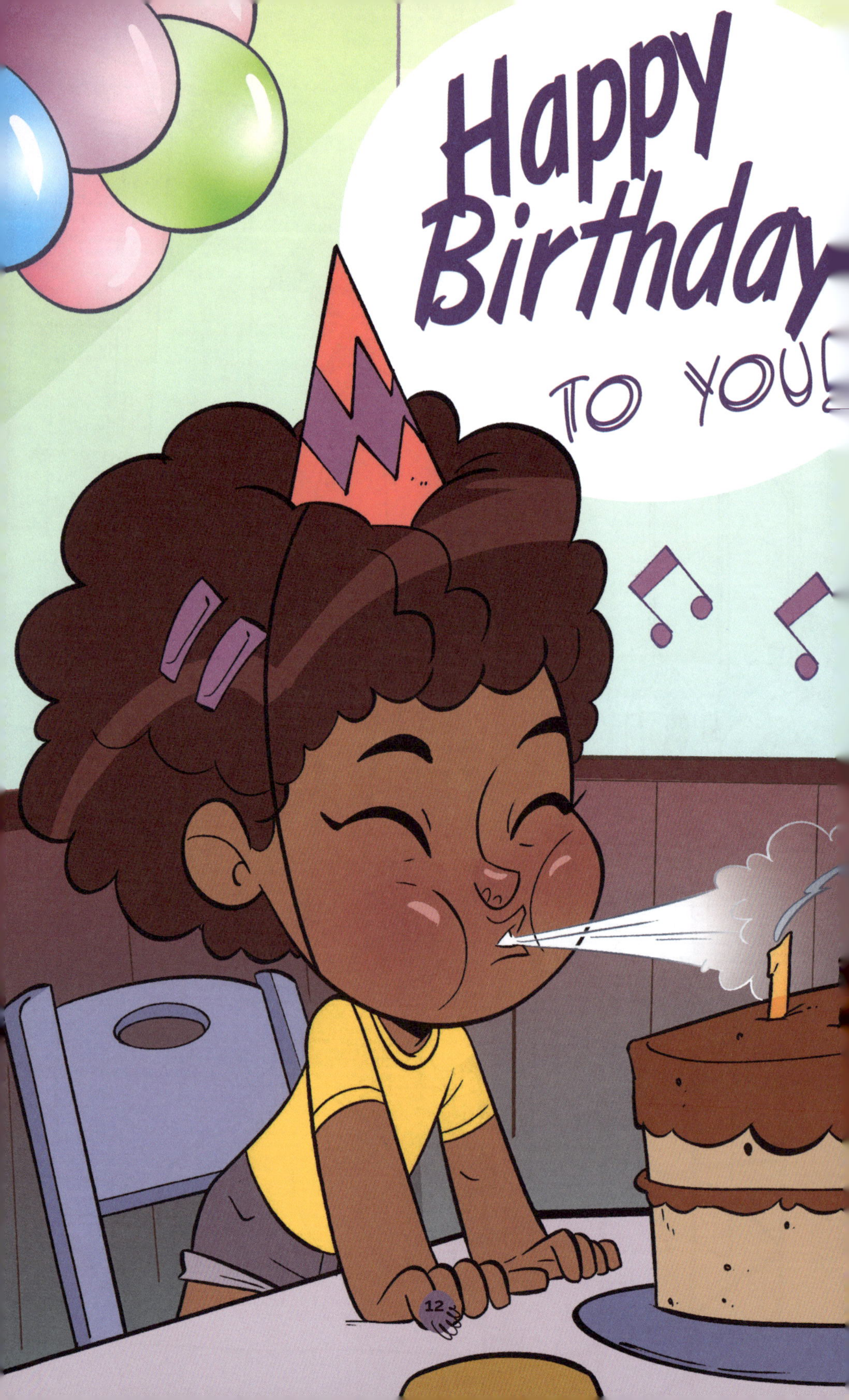
Happy Birthday
TO YOU!

We will sing **Happy Birthday!**
And have cake and candy.

Are you ready?

I am!

Let's have fun!